The
Alphabet
as
Resistance

Laws Against Reading,
Writing and Religion
in the Slave South

JERRY CUNNINGHAM

Dedication

To my daughters

Contents

I. Introduction

The slave power, as it was known in the nineteenth century, was the collection of slaveowners in the South that rose up to control the making of laws within the slave states. The laws about slavery were set forth in slave codes in each state; those codes were detailed rules on day to day control of the slaves. In all matters, the slaveowner was in charge of slave management, and responsible for it. These were times when the towns and cities had head counts in the low thousands, and farm life dominated the economic life of the region. It is not surprising that the state laws concerned farm life, but because farm life was dominated by slavery, it may be surprising to the reader just how detailed the laws were about controlling the slaves.

During the entirety of the slave centuries, whether under British rule or American.- right up until the Civil War from 1861 to 1865, the slaves were controlled by one main rule. Local men, always much poorer than the plantation owners, saw to it that the one main rule was enforced, especially at night, without a police force. The rule was that slaves could not leave the farms and plantations without a written pass from the owner, his family or an overseer. The local men, on horseback, were called the "patrols." The punishments for violating the pass rule were set forth in the slave codes in an arithmetic of cruelty, specifying the exact number of lashes that were to be inflicted on a slave caught without a pass. By definition, the patrols had charge of the roads and hunted and ensnared escapees in known hideouts in the hills or swamps. By definition also, the slaveowner had charge of his plantation as a miniature despotism.

During the chief time-frame of this book, 1830-1850, slavery expanded, especially in the Deep South - into the heart of South Carolina, out to the coast of Georgia, and into the then-new states of Mississippi, Louisiana, Arkansas, Florida, Alabama and Texas. Because importing slaves on the high seas was banned in Congress in 1808, the slaves for the expanding cotton and sugar plantations came, at first, from the South Carolina and Georgian coasts, and then bred in the 'border states' of Virginia, Kentucky and Tennessee and sold to the expanding new South. In the half-century before the Civil War, perhaps a million men, women and children were forced from their farms on the coasts or in the 'border states' and sent into gang slavery on the cotton and sugar plantations - a massive, modern Exodus towards conditions known for their cruelty. The plantations were planted on land freshly wrested from the Indians; in the 1830's, the common sight of wigwams along the rivers was eliminated, for the cotton age met the stone age, and the cotton age won.

Yet, the expanding cotton and sugar plantations on what had been, until the 1830's, Indian land, were not just new farms, they were new types of farms, where the crops required year-round labor, and that labor was most profitable when worked in gangs of dozens or even hundreds. The owners of these new plantations were the slave power - they had the wealth, they had the slaves, they had the local laws, and they increasingly had the national power to protect and expand slavery into new territories. The slave power was comprised of plantation owners that numbered say, ten thousand, out of the 300,000 Southern slaveowners.

Slavery was not just inseparable from government; it was a function of government. One tool of slavery, forced mass illiteracy, was mandated during the 1830-1850 time period by the governments of the slave states in a manner that had never been seen before. The patrols were required by law to enforce the anti-literacy laws, as well as new laws against gatherings of slaves and free blacks for any reason, including religious ones. The patrols were, unlike prior centuries, made to enforce these laws on the plantations themselves, by searching the rows of slave huts for slaves without passes and contraband, such as spelling books or newspapers. The new type of plantation, the large-scale, gang-slave cotton or sugar plantation, placed slaves together in massive numbers, especially males, and this type of farm required more controls; the slave codes were tightened to provide those controls. In Louisiana, two-thirds of the slaves on the sugar cane plantations were male.

Prior to 1830, it was common in the South for anti-slavery views to be discussed and considered by the churches, newspapers, and local groups. The gradual abolition of slavery was discussed all the time; it was a main theme written sub rosa into the Constitution of 1787. In fact, the question, "will slavery ever end?" was addressed constantly before the Constitution was written, yet the word "slavery" was kept out of the document. One provision says that the importation of "such persons" - slaves - could not be banned by Congress for twenty years. Another says that the Constitution could not be amended to ban the importation of slaves, again for twenty years. Six of twenty-eight clauses of the Constitution of 1787 directly concerned slavery; others did so indirectly. The Constitution, in large part, was originally a slavery-protection scheme.

After 1830, driven by isolated rebellion, the need to protect the slaveowners from their large, condensed, male workforces and by the emergence of a new, loud Northern campaigner - the sudden-abolitionist - the anti-literacy laws were joined with anti-assembly laws barring gatherings of free blacks or slaves for any reason, including religious ones, or limiting their numbers, or requiring white supervision. The minds of free blacks - who were never more than 2 or 3 percent of the black population - and slaves needed to be controlled with greater ferocity than in any other period during the centuries of slavery. Soon, the large slaveowners, as they gathered power over all political opposition in the South, added anti-abolitionist laws to the anti-literacy laws and anti-assembly laws. The growing power and paranoia of the large slaveowners was reflected, too, in a plan to control the minds of the slaves by allowing Protestant missionaries on the plantation. This "Mission to the Slaves" spanned only two decades but reached into the largest plantations, most of which had been no-go areas for religious instruction in prior years, and taught the slaves the basic tenets: obey your masters and do not steal.

For a reaction set in across the South, led by the slave power, after 1830. The reaction took the form of increased repression of free blacks in the towns and cities, including head taxes, deportations, white-sponsor requirements, job limitations, elimination of voting rights, and registration rules. The enhancements in the total control of the slaves by a labyrinth of acerbic laws - anti-literacy, anti-assembly, anti-religion - was one form of the reaction. Another form was the political domination of the governorships and legislatures across the South, to the exclusion of small slaveholders, independent farmers, and the white tradesmen of the towns and cities. The reaction also took the form of domination of the churches by the slaveholders, and, in the 1840's, the Southern churches divorced from their Northern brethren.

In the main, the reaction was a reflection of both the need for control of the isolated workforces on the large plantations and of the sinister, growing political power of the largest slaveowners over other whites in the South and in the halls of the U.S. Senate. Early roots of the reaction of 1820-1850 include Haiti: the slaves of Haiti fought a war against their French masters for thirteen years, resulting in a victory over Napoleon and Haitian independence in 1803. This frightened the U.S. slaveowners. Precedent from abroad was bad news: the British ended their ancient Atlantic trade in slaves in 1808. But most importantly, slave revolts in the South, small in scale but provoking wide scale fear among the slaveholders across the region (Charleston, South Carolina,, 1822; Southampton, Virginia, 1831) drove the reaction and resulted in a storm of furious laws. Sudden-abolitionist ideas grew into a movement in the North in the 1830's and were blamed for all new repressive laws and customs. The political possibilities of extending slavery into the newly-acquired U.S. territories - the entire Midwest by purchase from France in 1803, Texas by war in 1845, California and the territories of Utah and New Mexico by treaty in 1848 - fueled the reaction, too. Were these new territories to be parceled into multiple slave states? The plan for Texas, for example, was that it would eventually house five separate slave states, each, of course, with two U.S. senators. Also, would the Army be used for foreign conquest for the sake of new slave lands, like Texas had been, and would the Navy be used to take Cuba and Central America? These federal subjects are outside the scope of this book, but the effects of the reaction reached down from the height of the U.S. Senate and the war plans of the generals into the slave codes of each state, and from there into the humble, defenseless huts of the slaves.

The huts may have been defenseless, but the slaves weren't. Everywhere and everyday the slaves resisted slavery, from taking food - stealing it, in the eyes of the slaveowners and their theological assistants - to sabotage, to running away. This book is about two types of resistance by slaves, and their unsung majesty: secretly learning to read and write and secretly gathering to pray in order to exercise the rituals of a shadow religion.

II. The Pass, the Patrol, the Power to Whip

A. Overview

In the pre-Civil War South, the laws recorded the great, white fears of the time: insurrection by the slaves as a whole, revenge by the individual slave, and escape of slaves. The system of everyday control of slaves was the same throughout the slave states: slaveholders, according to law, could not allow their slaves to leave the plantation, especially at night, without a pass written by the slaveholder, a member of his family or his overseer. If a slave visited another plantation with a pass, he commonly was to "show himself to the employer or overseer," as a manual of the time said. The state laws - the slave codes - mandated that local patrols were to be organized, to check for passes, find runaways, and locate and break-up unlawful assemblies of slaves or free blacks.

These laws were part of the vast iron web of restraint built up over centuries against slaves. This web of restraint got the thickest, and the cruelest, during the dramatic employment of slave gangs on the cotton, rice and sugar plantations during the main time period of this book, 1830 to 1850.

These laws were long enforced; for example, North Carolina established patrols in 1753, Texas as late as 1846. The earliest law requiring slaveowners to provide passes to slaves who left the plantation was passed in Virginia in 1680. South Carolina, a state with a majority of blacks, had a pass law by 1686. The South Carolina law at first empowered whites to apprehend any slave off the plantation without a pass; within a few years, the law made it the duty of all whites to apprehend such slaves. As early as 1720 in South Carolina the law and practice was that "any person seeing a negro or slave out of his master's plantations without a ticket or in company with a white person was empowered to correct such servant by whipping, not exceeding twenty lashes." Slaves needed a pass - a "ticket" - in North Carolina to leave a plantation as early as 1715.

In 1759, Georgia's Royal Legislature passed a law that strengthened night watches in Savannah. The watchmen had to bring as kit "a good gun, a Cartridge box with six Cartridges at least filled with good Gun powder and a Ball in each." Slaves found without a "Tickett" were to be seized and apprehended; the punishment was to be "whipped on the bare back by one of the Watchmen with a Cow Skin Switch or horse Whip not exceeding twenty lashes." The watchmen were given the "full power" to enter any "disorderly tipling house" run by whites or free blacks to find slaves, and to whip them once found.

The criminal laws of the time - furious, written utterances of the slave power - protected whites only: assault and battery, false imprisonment, kidnapping, mayhem, torture, rape and murder were daily and hourly crimes against masses of slave men, women and children across the South, but there was no remedy, no protection by the law - the owners and the patrols were the lawmen. Rape was a daily event, and often not hidden, indeed shown off. An "illicit connection with their female slaves" was once deplored in Virginia, a British traveler was told in 1804, but by that year the attitudes of whites had long-since changed. By then, "there were but few slave-holders in the place who were free from guilt" and sex with slave women was "thought but little of. Such was the brutality and hardness of heart which this evil produced, that many amongst them paid no more regard to selling their own children, by their female slaves, or even their brothers and sisters, in the same line, than they would do to the disposal of a cow or a horse, or any other property in the brute creation."

The criminal laws protected whites from slaves. All states, early on, passed laws making it a crime punishable by whipping to hit a white person; South Carolina did so in 1740. The episodic occasions when slaveowners were punished for excessive violence just proved the rule: the slaves had nowhere to go, and no one to turn to.

The heyday of the patrols was 1820-1860, a period of rapid growth of slavery throughout the slave states. This was door to door control, and the laws and practices of the patrols governed the conduct of free blacks as well as slaves. "No two people who had the slightest tinge of color in their faces dared to be seen talking together." In the largest cities - New Orleans, Mobile, Savannah, Charleston, Richmond, Baltimore, Richmond, Louisville and St. Louis - slaves had dramatically more freedom than plantation slaves, though the slaves of the cities lived under a curfew and pass system and also faced irons, the lash and the public whipping post at the guardhouse and workhouse. The formal police forces - constables by day and a watch by night - of the cities had staffs measured in the dozens, though Charleston was an outlier with a force of 100, along with 60 members of the state guard and white militias. Thus, "[a]t any one time one might stop a black, ask for his papers, and frisk his clothing. A small matter or a slight infraction could end in a trip to jail. Resistance was foolish, an attempt to run away even worse." Slaves and free blacks in the cities, after the night watchman grabbed them, then faced courts where they had no rights and were sentenced to the lash. Mobile's Mayor's Court listed the numbers of lashes for each offense: 10 for getting drunk at Christmas; 15 for "impudence"; 25 for "insolent language"; 25 for being "out of place." More serious matters were dealt with by the auction-block and a grim return to the cotton and cane fields, or the gallows.

The true work of the patrols was done, however, in the countryside. Patrols stopped blacks on the roads, monitored the woods and cypress swamps, checked the train tracks and searched the homes of slaves. The patrols broke up gatherings deemed to be "unlawful assemblies" and looked for slaves without passes, runaways and those little, but deadly and civilization-ending things that the slaves should not possess: any written note or document, silverware, guns, gunpowder, shot, or jars of preserves.

A popular author of books on the South observed in 1860: "Yet the security of the whites is in much less degree contingent on the action of the patrols than upon the constant, habitual and instinctive surveillance of all white people over all black." That observer noted that in the towns and cities (he spoke of his visit to Charleston) there is "police machinery such as you never find in towns under free government: citadels, sentries, passports, grape-shotted cannons, and daily public whippings of the subjects for accidental infractions of police ceremonies." He continued: "I found that more than half the inhabitants of this town were subject to arrest, imprisonment, and barbarous punishment, if found in the streets without a passport after the evening 'gunfire'."

The method throughout the slave states was the same in the towns and cities: a curfew was enacted for slaves, and no slave without a pass, or who was not accompanied by a white person, could be in the streets after the curfew.

B. The Laws of Tennessee as an Example of a Slave Code

The detailed laws of the State of Tennessee on the subjects of patrols and the smothering of activities that could lead to insurrections are typical of the state laws about patrols.

First of all, a slave needed a pass (often called certificates, or tickets, or passports) to leave "the premises where he is appointed to live." Slaves could not keep weapons, including guns; could not hunt, even for the master, without strict controls; could not assemble "in unusual numbers, or at suspicious times and places" or have "spiritous liquors" in their possession. "Insulting or provoking language used by a slave to any white person" was a crime. Conspiracy to rebel or commit insurrection was punishable by death.

Tennessee's law said that patrols were to work "every night" unless "impracticable." The patrols were told to patrol areas where it was suspected that slaves "frequented" without the slaveholder's permission; search for guns and weapons each month; search "all Negro houses and suspected places" and whip those without passes up to fifteen lashes; apprehend those without passes and return them to the owner; and capture runaways. The patrols, covering the roads, made escape difficult. Alice Green, a former slave, said, "Lordy Honey! How could dem [slaves] run off to de North when dem patterollers and their hounds was waitin' to run 'em down and beat 'em up?" If slaves had religious instruction, it was to be told to obey - no wonder that, to many slaves, running away to freedom "seemed like stealing," as a former slave later wrote.

Other states had similar, exacting laws; Kentucky early made it unlawful for a plantation owner to allow five or more slaves "other than his own" on the property. A slave or freeman who was part of such an unlawful assembly, "or who shall be found strolling about from one plantation to another, without a pass from his or her master, mistress or overseer" was to get up to ten lashes on "his or her bare back, at the discretion of the captain of the patrol." Arkansas passed the identical law in 1825. Florida banned "travel in the high road" for groups of over seven male slaves without the presence of a white person. Mississippi kept its clock ticking: slaveowners, or their overseers, who allowed pass-less slaves on their plantation "above four hours at any one time" were fined.

C. Examples of City Ordinances and County Laws

The muddy cities of the slave states added another layer of laws. Charleston - a major Southern city of the time with 30,000 inhabitants - criminalized the assembly or meeting of more than "seven grown negroes" without the presence of a white person. But what if a white citizen wanted to hire, say, a dozen slaves that he did not own? Or the owner of a slave wanted him to work for someone else for money? One method was to make it mandatory for the hired-out slaves to wear badges "on some visible part of his or her dress." The badges were paid for by the owners, and lasted for a year.

Another method, used in Virginia, was to register the slaves for work outside of the city cutting down trees in the "Dismals" - the marshy areas. "Before leaving, they are all examined and registered at the Court House; and 'passes,' good for a year, are given to them, in which their features and the marks upon their persons are minutely described."

Cities and states said that slaves needed to carry passes, but could not carry other items. Augusta, Georgia had the following law:

No slave or free person of color shall
walk with a cane, club, or stick [. . .] nor
smoke a pipe or cigar in any street, lane,
alley or other public place, under a
penalty of not exceeding 25 lashes.

Augusta's laws also said that lights in slave quarters
were prohibited after 10:00 p.m.

Other cities controlled slaves and free blacks
with equally meticulous detail. Charleston banned
blacks from "whooping or hallooing anywhere in the
city, or making a clamorous noise or of singing aloud
any indecent song."

Common practices filled the void where no
laws were passed. Solomon Northrup, the man who
wrote *Twelve Years a Slave,* who was held near
Louisiana's Red River and the surrounding bayous,
said that the slaves were "not allowed to learn the art
of swimming, and are incapable of crossing the most
inconsiderable stream."

The patrols might get tough because the slave
dressed too well on his way to church. Moses Grandy,
a former slave, recalled: "If a negro has given offence
to the patrol, even by so innocent a matter as dressing
tidily to go to a place of worship, he will be seized by

one of them, and another will tear up his pass; while one is flogging him, the others will look another way."

Times of excitement, such as in Maryland around 1820, brought out the patrols. "[A]fter 1820, any justice in Anne Arundel, Calvert, Charles, Prince George's and St. Mary's counties was empowered, on the application of three judicious persons, to call out patrolling parties to search the neighborhood, for from four to eight hours, to see that the negroes were at home and orderly." Also in Maryland: "especially in times when insurrections were talked of and patrollers were more or less about, the customary salutation of a white to any strange and suspicious looking black: 'Well, boy, whom do you belong to?' sometimes ended in an unpleasant delay" for free blacks.

In times of excitement, even Christmas brought no relief to the pass laws. The whites of Sumner County, Tennessee, in 1856, learned of a foiled plot by slaves. They met and resolved "[t]hat during the Christmas holidays no slave be permitted to leave his master's premises, unless on business of the master or owner, and with his written permission, specifying the time, place, and business." "Each master" was told to "patrol his own premises, see that his own slaves remain home at night and on the Sabbath; and that other negroes do not congregate with his."

The patrols would also search the slaves' cabins for passless boyfriends and husbands, guns, bullets, shot, knives or other weapons, and for other contraband, defined to include any written note or document of any kind. The patrols looked for unlawful assemblies - prayer meetings, get togethers, parties, hiding spots - broke them up, and imposed whippings as punishment, as shall be discussed in Chapter VII. The patrol system lasted for two centuries throughout the pre-war South and was at its most intense where slavery was deepest - Virginia and North Carolina, and most especially South Carolina, Georgia, Alabama and Mississippi.

The patrols were "a system of espionage" across the entire Southern countryside. Who were the patrollers? They were "non-slaveholders, small farmers, merchants, professional men, mechanics, overseers, and others." A common vision of the patrollers: "The clatter of their horses' hoofs dashing by can be heard at all hours of the night, and frequently they may be seen driving a slave before them, or leading him by a rope fastened around his neck to his owner's plantation."

Over time, the patrols were folded under the county militias, or patrollers became exempt from militia duty, or the patrols reported to the county courts. The patrols became a paid, compulsory service for white males. The patrollers took an oath and occasionally had badges; they were paid by the county or city. The patrols were made of armed men with revolvers and rifles, on horseback, accompanied by dogs, and carrying "great big torches of fire." If a slave "got out without a pass, dey set de hounds on you; and de patrollers'd tear you up too, if you stayed out too late," recalled Carrie Davis, a former Alabama slave. Without a pass, "dem Patterrollers would have 'em a-runnin' through the woods jes' lack dey was a lot of deer," said former Alabama slave Martha Jackson.

The dogs were notorious. The mother of Evie Harris worked as a housemaid, and one day her mother ran away. The patrol "hunted her with dogs. Them dogs went straight to the ditch where my mother was hid, and before the men could get to them, they had torn the clothes off her and had bitten her all over." Books were contraband. "Us couldn't leave de plantation without a pass; and you better not let 'em catch you wid a book," Carrie Davis said.

The patrollers - called 'paddy rollers' and similar names by the slaves - were also ready to whip; the "patrol was in the habit of traversing the streets with cowskins." The slaveowners were not the patrollers by and large; indeed, their interests often conflicted, as the slaveowners did not want their slaves damaged, and there were a number of cases where a slaveowner sued patrollers for 'trespass' when the patrollers beat and whipped a slave into disability, or killed him.

The patrols, mandatory for white men, were thought to be an effective way to avoid the tyranny of a standing army: "With us every citizen is concerned in the maintenance of order, and in promoting honesty and industry among those of the lowest class who are our slaves; and our habitual vigilance renders standing armies, whether of soldiers or policemen, entirely unnecessary. Small guards in our cities, and occasional patrols in the country, ensure us a repose and security known nowhere else." This vigilance by all whites was reflected in laws, like that of Jefferson City, Missouri, requiring all citizens to help the patrols if called upon. The normal fact about slaveholders: "Their safety depends upon their vigilance." Thus, the patrols were everywhere:

Jericho, Jericho, I been to Jerusalem
Patrol aroun' me.
Thank God he no catch me.
Went to the meetin'
Met brother Hercules.
What d'ya think he tell me?
Tell me for to turn back.
Jump along Jericho.

Since patrols prowled mainly at night, except at times of rebellions or rumors of rebellions, the slaves and the patrollers needed to know when the curfew began. "The slaves must all be at their homes precisely at eight o'clock, p.m. At this hour the drums beat in the cities, as a signal for every slave to be in his den. In the country, the signal is made by firing guns, or some other way by which they may know the hour when to be at home." Augusta, Georgia's law said: "No slave or free person of color shall be absent from his or her house 15 minutes after the bell shall have been rung, without a sufficient pass, under the penalty of 25 lashes."

III. The Hardening of Slavery after 1830: The Reaction Takes Hold

A. The Profitability of Cotton Gives Rise to the Slave Power

There were two major plots by U.S. slaves before the 1830's. Thereafter, there were endless rumors of small-scale rebellions throughout the South, and endless fears of a large-scale one. First, in Virginia, there was the Gabriel uprising in the capital city of Richmond in 1800; though no whites died, the laws then began to get more strict. Virginia's 1804 law targeted religion: it banned the "nighttime religious meetings of slaves."

There was other news at the time, emanating from the French slave-holdings in the Caribbean. The slaves of Haiti rebelled and fought for and obtained control of large parts of Haiti. The French, under instructions from Napoleon, sought to retake Haiti in

1803-04 from republican slave generals, using 35,000 troops. Twenty-eight thousand French troops died in the effort, mostly of disease, along with 19 white French generals. The French were defeated, and the independent Republic of Haiti was formed in 1804, with a constitution that banned slavery. As a direct result of the Haitian Revolution, French Louisiana - not to mention the bulk of today's Midwest - was sold cheaply by France to the U.S. All of this followed thirteen years of fighting begun and led by runaway slaves in the Haitian mountains. A generation later, preacher Nat Turner in Southampton County, Virginia led a two-day uprising, often called "the Turner Cataclysm," that killed 50-60 whites, including women and children. Nat Turner could read - mainly the Bible. The original plot was set for July 4th, 1831 but delayed until August. After the first murders by the rebels, slaves joined them for their attack on the county seat, Jerusalem. The plotters traveled twenty miles before their defeat. "The case of Nat Turner warns us. No black man ought to be permitted to turn a Preacher through the country," warned a Virginia newspaper. The post-Nat Turner repression of Southern blacks was total.

The blacks of the South in 1831 faced three daggers. The first dagger was a growing fear of insurrection and hatred of abolitionists, accompanied by the growing political power of the slaveholders, especially the large ones.

The second dagger was a rapid, five year almost-doubling of the price of cotton, from 1830 to 1835, and an almost-doubling of the price of slaves. Indeed, the price of slaves nearly tripled in the lowlands of South Carolina and Georgia from 1830 to 1837. The slaveholders of the Deep South were about to find that additions to their chief asset, their total number of slaves, were now more costly by the month. Slavery, driven by the expansion of large cotton farms into the new states of Alabama, Mississippi and Louisiana and later into Texas and other lands west of the Mississippi River, was about to make a lot of planters rich. And to make them more valuable, the slaves would be worked even harder, with a new "stress on clock time."

The third dagger was the passage of the Abolition of Slavery Bill in Britain's Parliament in 1833. Britain's slaveholders in the Caribbean - Jamaica, Antigua, Barbados, Grenada, Guyana,

Trinidad, St. Lucia, Tobago - held onto every acre under the Abolition of Slavery Bill, and were generously paid by the British government for their loss of property. The Southern slaveholders of the U.S., more aware of the British-Caribbean emancipation of the 700,000 slaves there than anyone else, feared the British example, and set out to repress even the idea of it in the South, and resist even the idea of it in Congress.

By the 1830's, the slave power was about to reach its height, where it would stay until the Civil War in 1861. Truly, a Georgian minister wrote, then "the slave power wrenched from the soil the last dollar it could yield, to buy another negro, to open another field, to make more cotton, to buy still another negro!" As King Cotton's profits grew, the value of the work of the slaves grew: picking, seed-cleaning in gins, and packing. The laws that repressed all blacks grew too, as did the reach of the patrols and the police forces of the towns and cities, and the slaveholders' political dominance and unity. In the mix, the price of slaves rose, following the macabre logic of the old rule. "The old rule of pricing a negro by the price of cotton by the pound - that is to say, if cotton is worth twelve cents, a negro man is worth $1200.00" Slave labor became, in the main, gang labor on massive cotton farms.

Cotton supplied a world market with cheap cloth. "Probably not one-tenth of the white people of the South were dependent for a livelihood on the raising of cotton; but fully three-fourths of the slave labor was applied to that crop." The fleecy staple of cotton was shipped in heavy bales on flatboats by river and then on ship across the Atlantic to the growing cotton port of Liverpool; then, in Lancashire, it was made into cloth, where spinning and weaving mills had become industrial. The cotton industry of Britain employed four million. Or the bales were shipped by river or, after 1830, by rail to Southern cotton ports - Charleston, Savannah, Mobile, Galveston and New Orleans - and from those ports on to the port of New York and then by rail to the cotton mills of New England.

Cotton could be farmed on almost all the tillable land of the South. The planting of the popular 'sea-island' cottons spread from the upper and middle regions of South Carolina and the pinelands of Georgia "westward into the 'back country' of the Carolinas, across the pine hills and prairies of Georgia and Alabama, took complete possession of the alluvial lands along the Mississippi and Red rivers, and by 1860 were laying claim to the great central region of Texas." Mass gang slavery not only spread to Texas, but chimerical plans and calls were made to annex Cuba and Nicaragua. In the 1830's, the rich pinelands of the Carolinas, Georgia, and Texas, the coastal lands, prairie lands and river bottoms of Louisiana with its 'Gulf cotton,' the river lands and valleys of Tennessee, and the prairies of Mississippi and Alabama became ground zero for planting cotton. Plantations mushroomed along the rich bottom lands of the Mississippi and Red rivers.

Virginia, Maryland, North Carolina, Kentucky, Tennessee, Missouri, Delaware - the 'border states' - had much smaller proportions of slaves in their populations than the Deep South of South Carolina, Georgia, Alabama, Mississippi and Louisiana. The 'border states' and the District of Columbia became slave exporters - slave breeders - to the Deep South during this time. That is, the farmers of the 'border states' grew crops of humans on their weakening tobacco and corn farms and sold them, in coffles, southwards, either by foot and wagon, by river steamer, or on ships out of the ports of Virginia and

Maryland, with the leg-shackled men and women chained by arm together in pairs, marching in double-file. This business of growing slaves and selling them from the Upper South to the Deep South worked like this. A shipper-slavedriver "goes annually to the Southwestern States, to make his contracts with those planters there who are in want of slaves for the next season." There was a division of labor. "The women and grown-up girls are usually sold into the cotton-growing States, the men and the boys to the rice and sugar plantations."

South Carolina and Georgia are sister states, separated by the Savannah River. The deeper that slavery expanded into the swamps and rice paddies of South Carolina and Georgia, or the cane fields of Louisiana, the greater the death-rate of slaves due to constant malaria, and outbreaks of cholera, smallpox and yellow fever. The high death rate of slaves was well known. A traveler wrote,

> Great numbers are . . . absorbed by South Carolina and Georgia, where the cultivation of rice thins the black population so fast, as to render a constant fresh supply of Negroes indispensable in

order to meet increasing demand for that great staple production of the country. [. .] During certain seasons of the year, I am informed, all the roads, steam-boats, and packets are crowded with troops of Negroes on their way to the great slave market of the South.

The high profits from slave-selling after 1830 meant that field hands were imported from the slave states further north; it also meant that the men and boys - especially the men and boys - were sold off in droves by their town and city owners into gang slavery in the countryside. The sell-off was so stark that "it produced an increasing surplus of female slaves remaining in towns." In the towns, "[a]s early as 1820 women had begun to outnumber men; by 1860, the difference was striking." The pattern continued for decades. "On the eve of the war almost every Southern town had a . . . glaring shortage of [black, slave] men." The shortages of black men were obvious among free blacks as well; in New Orleans, for example, there were 1750 more free females than males. The key scholar of slavery in the cities, Richard Wade, concluded that "[i]n the cities, the colored women, both bond and free, easily outnumbered the men." A traveler wrote in his diary in 1859, that "[t]he slaves in the cities, working in the midst of the conversation of white men, listen eagerly, and gain some information." This, the traveler wrote, "has alarmed their masters, and they are sending them off, as fast as possible, to the plantations where, as in a tomb, no sight or sound of knowledge can reach them."

Cotton and slavery were twins because cotton required hand work for planting and harvesting, was cultured by labor for 9 of 12 months of the year, and was cleaned in the cotton gins and baled into bales of 300 pounds, and so required a steady, permanent, strong workforce. The crop, grown in the South in the times of slavery without fertilizer and without crop rotation, exhausted the land; thus, new land was always sought. The land, to the planters, was a "perishable or movable property," to be "worn out, not improved"; the planters often abandoned their fields, chained slaves in tow, and headed for virgin lands, at first in west Georgia or Alabama or Tennessee, and later in Mississippi or Arkansas or Texas. The property that the planters invested in was not land, it was the slave. For the Cotton Belt, the "plan of planting" was "simply to work lands, negroes and mules to the top of their bent," wrote a South Carolina newspaper. The sentimental life of the slaveowner is hopelessly overrated in U.S. movies; more candor was given by an Englishwoman in her account of a time spent on her husband's estates in Georgia. She wrote of "the shaggy unkempt grounds we passed through to approach the house; the ruinous, rackrent, tumble-down house itself; the untidy, slatternly, all but beggarly appearance of the mistress of the mansion herself." Indeed, Southern cotton planters were known for their laziness and lack of skill by other Southern farmers. A Mississippi farmer wrote in 1852 of the cotton men. "What did you see in your last summer's tour? Did you see any little twelve by six log cribs covered with four-feet board? Any fodder-stacks, with the Mississippi mud? A pasture for calves without grass or water? Sheep with one-half of each without wool? Fences as if the rails had fallen from above, and happened to light upon each other? Men riding with rope bridle-reins?"

Slaves, during the mild Southern winters, cleared the timberland by slashing and so killing the trees, cutting down and burning the smaller ones, rolling and burning the large ones in heaps, and breaking up the ground with cheap, crude iron tools for planting as early as February. Large plantations, once cleared, were a natural fit to the cotton crop. "As a single laborer can cultivate successfully only from five to ten acres of cotton, while in Indian corn, for example, he can cultivate thirty or forty acres, it is obvious that laborers can be more compactly massed, and more of them brought under the eye of a single overseer in the cotton fields, than when they are employed in cultivating corn." Gang labor ruled the Cotton Belt.

Georgia is a special case in the rise of King Cotton and the relentless rise of mass gang slavery. The numbers tell part of the story: there were 30,000 blacks in Georgia in 1790, 100,000 by 1810, 200,000 by 1820, and 500,000 at the start of the Civil War. For it is in the lands of south and southwest Georgia where the Creek Indians had lived for centuries, hunting its woods, and in those lands, with their rolling hills extending into the fearsome, hot, red clay expanses below Macon, and between the Chattahoochee and Flint rivers, that cotton was to make its pre-War stand. West Georgia had less than 200 slaves in 1800; by 1840 it had 156,000, a figure that doubled again by the eve of the Civil War. There would have been no Georgian mass gang slavery in astounding numbers but for cotton, and cotton needed new fields at all times. The answer was the removal of the Creek Indians in central and southern Georgia by fraud, theft, gun, state law and national politics.

Much of the old-growth forests of pine, oak, ash hickory and poplar could and would be felled by the slaves; the thick black soil beneath the forests, and adjacent swampland, turned to cotton fields. The 1820's and 1830's were the time of King Cotton's great expansion westward - and westward meant away from Georgia's coast, and away from Virginia and the Carolinas, headstrong into Indian land. The emigrants included small farmers from other lands, pioneers without slaves. The slaveowners, too, were considered to be pioneers. A British traveler in 1846 sailed on a steamer along the Gulf shore from Mobile to New Orleans, and he met slaveowners traveling to Texas with their slaves. One of the slaveowners had settled in Alabama, and left for Texas. The traveler described the restless slaveowner, referring to the "years of labour" - of the slaves.

> He was, I found, one of those resolute pioneers of the wilderness, who, after building a log-house, clearing the forest,

and improving some hundred acres of wild ground by years of labour, sells the farm and migrates again to another part of the uncleared forest, repeating this operation three or four times in the course of his life, and, though constantly growing richer, never disposed to take his ease.

Who moved westward into what became known as the Black Belt? At first, as a newspaper of the time said, "cotton land speculators thicker than locusts in Egypt." Then squatters, outlaws, slaveowners, former overseers, small farmers and poor families looking to make it in the gold rush of the times, the freed-up free or near-free land of Georgia and Mississippi. The large slaveowners used up tobacco-land or corn-land in Virginia and Kentucky, or used up cotton-land in North Carolina or coastal and northern South Carolina and then took their slaves to better land, attracted by the fertile alluvial soil of the South Carolina and the Georgia lowlands, and the price: free, or nearly so. It was standard practice to send a part of the plantation "force" to the new lands to "colonize a plantation." Then, the escapee slaveholders might travel by flatboat with hundreds of slaves, along with food provisions for a year, horses, mules and cattle, and feed for the animals. New slaveowners also arrived as speculators from New England, and the slaves knew a rule that "persons who have been raised in the free States make the worst masters," a view shared by others.

The movement, over decades, of slaves from the coasts and the Upper South was massive. "Day after day the songs of the clank of chained feet marching from Virginia and Carolina to Georgia was heard in these rich swamp lands." And with the whites as they marched in triumph over red lands, came tightened, hardened slave codes, the laws against literacy and religion, and the patrols.

The Indian land was proudly made into the 'Egypt of the Confederacy' by white settlers, in a ferocious, gold-rush style. In Georgia, planters built their malarial palaces and parks; many of the most successful would live in Macon and Augusta, leaving the slaves alone with cruel overseers while the planters partied away at the steamy summers at resorts in Madison Springs. A visitor wrote his recollections of Georgia during this period.

Towards evening, we passed six wagons, conveying

ninety slaves belonging to General _____, removing from his plantation in Georgia, to his settlement on the Cahawba, in Alabama. I have already mentioned the numerous gangs which I continually fell in with on my route from the Atlantic to the Gulf of Mexico; and I have understood that from Maryland and Virginia alone, from 4000 to 5000 per annum are occasionally sent down to New Orleans: a place, the very name of which seems to strike terror into the slaves and free Negroes of the middle States.

B. The Cotton Slaveholders Expand by Taking the Land of the Indians

It was during the 1830's and 1840's that cotton moved westward, through Indian land. Wigwams hugged the riversides, and the woods were hunting grounds for deer and bear. Everywhere a settler, or a politician, went there were Indians. When you traveled through Georgia in the 1830's and 1840's, you traveled through the Indians. The new Governor of Georgia in 1837 got these traveling instructions for returning to town with his wife on a stagecoach: "we should go direct to Georgia by the McIntosh trail, through the Creeks, instead of the road by Benton court-house through the Cherokees." The couple chose to go through the hostile Creeks, who were facing impending removal: "we passed through the Creek wilderness."

In South Carolina, cotton spread from the farms of the coastal tidelands up the rivers into the uplands and finally into the center of the state. Cotton spread in Georgia from the coast, westward along the rivers into and across central Georgia and then into and across central Alabama and central Mississippi. The southern tip of Tennessee grew into cotton country. And the Mississippi Valley was about to be colonized: cotton spread along the great river from the plantations outside of Memphis down to the thick cotton regions of river-coast Mississippi and river-coast Arkansas, and down to the fertile, free or near-free lands above the Gulf of Mexico - the lower Mississippi. "The Indian title was extinguished" in the new cotton lands. The Indian lands were "conquered provinces, just opened to colonization." The Black Belt replaced the red one.

All along, hard-scrabble small farmers of South Carolina and Georgia, plowmen with no slaves or few, sold their lands and migrated, either northwards into Kentucky or Tennessee, or, in a rush of settlement deeper into Georgia and Alabama, or on, often by steamboat, towards the Mississippi Valley and Gulf. The small farmers were log-cabin settlers. The small farmers, who often owned no slaves, after long travels with only a single-shot rifle, a couple of mules, a crate of chickens and a bag of seed corn, cut out their clearings in the wilderness along the rivers feeding the lower Mississippi and set up modest cotton and corn farms.

Meanwhile, the old mansions of the large slaveholders of the cotton and rice farms along the coasts of Georgia and South Carolina sank into decrepitude, often abandoned, as were the fields; if still tilled, the ranks of the slaves were thinned as the slaves were sold or moved. All along, large slaveowners of Virginia, along with those of coastal, tidewater South Carolina and Georgia, bought up 'wildland' in the Deep - cotton - South and became absentee owners of their new farms and plantations, or ended up moving south, family, coffles of slaves and bloodhounds in tow. When the richer slaveholders or their sons or their overseers moved, they traveled around and through the forests of western Georgia, Alabama, and Mississippi. Those lands soon thickened with slaves. Further south, New Orleans became the noisiest market for slaves, taking in illegally imported ones and selling them to the new cotton men and the rice and sugar planters of Louisiana.

The richer the slaveholder the better the land that he bought to grow his cotton; he often drove out, by land purchase, the new small farmers, who ended up in the pine hills, having lost the battle between "pioneer and planter." The fertile 'buckshot' soils of the Deep South ended up owned by the big slaveholders; if the forests and woods had not already been cleared with flames and axes by a new small farmer, the slave burned and chopped down the trees and built the new 'big house.' To the west, Texas beckoned those small farmers; to the south, Cuba beckoned the big slaveholders, as did Central America.

The Governor of Georgia described a friend who had cotton fever.

> He married [in Georgia], cultivated a good plantation, and was growing rich in the country of his birth. The temptation

offered by the rich lands of Alabama, made him sell out. He acquired a large tract of land of the greatest fertility, and made money rapidly beyond example. His land increased in value, until he was offered ten dollars per acre for it. He heard that lands of equal production could be purchased in Texas for twenty-five cents per acre. He had left his house and family to search for lands in Texas, then inhabited by Spaniards and Indians, and was the receptacle of robbers and cutthroats of all sorts.

The Governor of Georgia also wrote in his memoirs of his talks in the 1830's with his friends in Montgomery, Alabama. He remembered that he would "listen to my Montgomery friends talking without ceasing of cotton, negroes, land and money. I had never myself bought negroes, or made profit out of their labor, accumulated any money by speculation, cultivated cotton, or been engaged in any way in the occupations which were stimulating them to incessant exertions."

The 'new country' of Alabama in the 1830's was described in a memoir this way: "Lots in obscure villages were held at city prices; lands, bought at the minimum cost of government, were sold at from thirty to forty dollars per acre, and considered dirt cheap at that." The new planter of Alabama lived hard and fast: he made "a permanent investment of one-half of his fortune in cigars, Champagne, trinkets, buggies, horses, and current expenses, including some small losses at poker."

The largest slaveowners became larger still. "The cheapness of land," wrote a British visitor in 1846, "caused by such rapid emigration to the South and West, and the frequent sales of the estates of insolvents, tempts planters to buy more land than they can manage themselves, which they must therefore give in charge to overseers. Accordingly, much of the property in Alabama belongs to rich Carolinians, and some wealthy slave-owners of Alabama have estates in Mississippi."

Indian removal, in the words of a British observer of the time, was "an extensive and systematic scheme of the Government, of transferring the Aborigines from the Eastern states to the Far-West."

Here is an account from around 1815 of early settling in Creek country. "The Alabama, Black Warrior Tombigbee, and Chattahoochee countries had all been acquired by conquest, and I was determined to seek a home in the wilderness." The account continued:

> Our company consisted of my father and mother and eight children, with six negroes; Joseph Bryan, my brother-in-law, and his wife and two negroes; my wife and me and two small sons and two negroes. We had good horses and wagons and guns and big dogs. We set out on the 10th of March, 1818. I felt as if I was on a big camp hunt. The journey, the way we traveled, was about 500 miles, all wilderness; full of deer and turkeys, and the streams were full of fish. We were six weeks on the road.

The land of Georgia, mostly Indian in 1820, was, by 1831, all Georgian land. In May, 1830, Congress passed the Indian Removal Act, empowering President Jackson, at his request, to remove the Indians of the Southeast - Creeks, Cherokee, Choctaw,

Chickasaw and Seminole – from their millions of acres of land to beyond the Mississippi river, to Oklahoma, by treaty. The Creeks lost a lot of land in Georgia in an 1814 treaty; a treaty in 1825 gave up all of their remaining Lower Creek land and a large swathe of Alabama. The Creek towns lined the Chattahoochee and Flint rivers; they would soon be emptied. The emigrations by drifting keelboats or on foot or by horse and wagon of men, women and children in the mud and rain to and across the Mississippi began in 1827; a larger party of 1,200 left in 1829 in the middle of a cholera epidemic. Alabama Creeks left in 1834 and 1835. A new treaty in 1832 came, the language clear: "The Creek tribe of Indians cede to the United States all their land, East of the Mississippi river." But the spring of 1836 brought the Second Creek War; the Creeks of today's Alabama rebelled and burned cotton plantations. The U.S. Army then deported the Creek prisoners and their families by marching them through Arkansas to Fort Gibson in Oklahoma; the remaining Creeks were marched westward in five large groups in the late summer of 1836. In 1837, the U.S. Army moved another group to New Orleans and onto steamboats up the Mississippi; one steamboat collision led to 300

Creek drownings. In the course of forty years, the Creeks lost 40 million acres - all of their ancient land - to the encroaching whites.

The lands of southwestern Georgia and central Alabama, the Choctaw land of central Mississippi, and the Chickasaw lands of northern Mississippi were transformed, in a decade, into the heartland of black slavery.

The Cherokees lived in today's north Georgia and Tennessee. The Cherokees lost it all in Georgia between 1827 and 1831 when Georgia's legislature extended its power over all of Indian land, and passed laws to abolish Indian laws and government, divide all Indian land into parcels, and give the parcels away for free by lottery to Georgia's whites. Cherokee land was signed away in a treaty opposed by the bulk of the tribe in 1835; the Cherokees were, under the treaty, to leave Georgia en masse within two years. Much of the Cherokee nation did not move, and their leaders protested to the federal government and brought court cases. In 1838, the U.S. Army, 7,000 strong, was sent into Cherokee land and, by gunpoint, forced four to five thousand Cherokees out of Georgia, across rivers, and into Oklahoma, a 500-mile journey, in the winter: it is known to history as "The Trail of Tears."

The Choctaws of Mississippi, who once possessed most of the soil of that state, suffered a similar fate. Large chunks of what would become the state of Mississippi - 4 million acres - were ceded by four treaties between 1801 and 1816; then, in 1820, a treaty with the U.S. government ceded 5.1 million acres of Mississippi in exchange for dry, rocky, sterile scrub brush land in Oklahoma. A treaty of 1825 required evacuation of Arkansas lands, but the white settlers opposed it, as it allowed the Choctaws to keep a tract 60 miles wide from the Arkansas River to the Red River. In Mississippi, in 1825-1827, the leaders of 23,400 Indians, a total higher than the Indian population of all the Northern states combined, resisted removal. In 1829, the government of Mississippi, by passing a law, took over all of the Indian lands of Mississippi and said that all Indians were now under its laws; failure to comply was a crime. After the federal Removal Act of 1830, treaty negotiations led to Choctaw agreement to give up all of their remaining 10.4 million acres east of the Mississippi. One third of the Choctaw were supposed to leave in each of the years 1831, 1832 and 1833; the

Choctaw people were unhappy with the deal. The whites of Mississippi, for their part, resisted allowing any remaining Choctaws to become citizens of their state. About 4,000 Choctaws left their ancestral lands in the wet fall of 1831, by wagon, by horseback, and by foot, and headed 300-500 miles for Mississippi ports, where they gathered to be removed by steamboat up the Mississippi, then on to the Arkansas River, and west into "Indian Territory," today's Oklahoma. Boats were forgotten; delays occurred; a typical ship carried 500 Choctaws. The deportees were sick, fearful, and starving; the last of the Choctaws did not arrive in Oklahoma until March, 1832: a five-month "Trail of Tears." The removal of the following year was also in winter, and took place during a fearful cholera epidemic, with cut rations; 1833's removal was also in winter. By the spring of 1834, 12,500 Choctaws had been removed from Mississippi; 6,000 remained in Mississippi believing they had treaty rights - they, too, would soon be forced out.

The removal of the Indian tribes for the sake of the expansion of slavery was complete. In 1849, a visitor to Savannah could write:

It is not more than twenty years since the last Indian tribes in Georgia were driven thence by an armed force; and I have heard eye-witnesses relate the scene, how on the morning when they were compelled to leave their huts, their smoking hearths, their graves, and were driven away, men, women, and children, as a defenseless herd, the air was filled with their cry of lamentation! Now no Indians are to be met with in

Georgia or Carolina, though in Alabama, the furthest state west, may still be found tribes of Choctaw and Chickasaw Indians. Lively picnics are now held on these ancient Indian mounds.

C. Slaves Replace the Indians; the Forests Are Felled

The 'border states' had become exporters of slaves. A Virginia professor, who spoke of abolishing slavery in 1831, wrote that "Virginia is in fact a negro-raising State for other States. She produces enough for her own supply, and six thousand for sale." In fact, in a slave exporting state like Maryland, "[t]he value of slaves in Maryland depends entirely on their value at New Orleans."

In Georgia, a German Duke visited and wrote his memoirs. Our Duke saw the farmers of Georgia heading in the dead of winter for the 'new country' of Alabama. After leaving a town in Georgia, the Duke was "traveling in the woods where there was little accommodation for travelers." Every night, he saw "bivouacs of wagoners or emigrants, moving to the western states - the backwoods." They were off to Alabama, "there to set themselves down and fall to hewing and building." Our Duke arrived in Alabama and there saw more white Georgian emigrants, who had bought land cheaply from the federal government. "The number of their negroes, wagons, horses, and cattle, showed that these emigrants were in easy circumstances."

Much of the daily work and implacable effort of the slaves is now forgotten. The captives tapped the trees for the endless barrels of turpentine sold by their masters. The slaves were the blacksmiths and ran the sawmills. The male and female slaves manned the plows, sowed the corn, wheat, and oats, raised the hogs and chickens, milked the cows and tended to the peach and fruit orchards, for their owners liked brandy. The slaves of cotton manned the gin-house and baling press in the heat. Yet, often forgotten, is the fact that the male slaves, by the tens of thousands, were loggers and carpenters. The male slaves hewed the timber for the houses, storerooms and mills. Aside from felling the forests, discussed below, slaves built all of the buildings from scratch: the smokehouse, the henhouse, the stable, the barn, the shed and silo, the workshop, the chapel and the school. And the 'big house.' And all of the fences. Near mountain streams, the slaves built and manned corn and flour mills. The slaves chopped wood for home use and, after 1810, for the river steamers, for wood was burned for steamer-fuel for many years before coal. The slaves constructed the railroads, built public and private roads and built the canals that connected the rivers.

'New' land in the 1830's and 1840's meant land newly cleansed of Indians. Yet, the Indians of the Southeast were not known for large farms, though they cleared forest to a limited extent for planting. Thus, the 'new' lands of the times were primeval forests of sycamores, amber-bearing poplars, tulip trees, oak, elms, and willows. For a cotton or other farm to exist, the forest had to be cleared of its heavy timber and its rocks. The slaves were forced to deforest the Southeast, one tree, and one rock, at a time.

From the beginning of slavery, the Southern plantations were cut from the primeval forests by the work of the slaves. There were two methods. The first method was to burn the acreage, allow the fallen trees to dry on the ground for months or even years, and then to pile them together - log rolling - and burn them again. It was common to see, in the South, acres and acres of forest burning night and day. The second, favored method, was girdling - killing the larger trees by stripping their bark around the trunk. Cotton could be planted underneath the dead trees within months. As the limbs fell and trees rotted or fell, they were burned, a few at a time. Throughout the South, reminiscences recorded the stark vision of the time: acres of burning forest and then tens of acres of dead, dark, leafless forest. Later, the brutal task of clearing the stumps by ax, oxen or muscle, was undertaken. East of the Mississippi, north and south, 100 million acres were cleared by the slaves by 1850.

The size of the achievement is one of the unsung labor-achievements of the male and female slaves. By contrast, white farmers with small farms might clear five acres of forest in a year. "But even farmers who specialized in clearing land for sale might count on two hundred acres or so of forest clearing as the labor of a lifetime."

Clearing forest with the help of slaves was done rapidly. One account of the times recorded the speed. "The land was cleared for about the space of an acre, and, in addition to the house, there were two outhouses; a stable, in which were the four mailhorses; and a granary. Thirteen days previously this was the middle of a wood, and not a tree was cut down!"

Another memory:

> I spoke to the overseer of the negroes. The man's employment I recognised from his whip, and from the use he made of it, in rousing up the negroes to make a fire. He told us that in the district where the plantation was situated, and where maize and cotton were planted, but a little time before there was nothing but forest. His employer had commenced in 1816, with

two negroes, and now he possessed one hundred and four, who were kept at work in clearing the wood, and extending the plantation.

A typical day was recorded in a planter's diary in Alabama. "14th Tuesday. The 4 double ploughs commenced listing up the corn land on the north side of the Graham field. The men rolling logs on the same place. The women setting fire to them."

It was written of Savannah in 1853 by a visitor: "Five-and-twenty years ago the ground on which the city stood, and the whole region around, was Indian territory and Indian hunting-ground. Where those wild dances were danced, and their wigwams stood, now stands Macon, with six thousand inhabitants, and shops and workshops, hotels and houses, and an annually increasing population."

D. The Churches Cave to the Slave Power

As the slave power grew, Southern anti-slavery movements collapsed. "Antislavery sentiment and organization in the early decades of the nineteenth century had flourished more in the South than in the largely apathetic North." Before 1830 the South had hundreds of antislavery organizations with thousands of members, although only in the Upper South and primarily in North Carolina and Tennessee. The anti-slavery forces, about 5,000 strong, faced a growing, intransigent defense of slavery; by 1831, Tennessee's 25 antislavery societies were gone. Across the South, anti-slavery societies dwindled, and their leaders migrated. The churches, meanwhile, faced popular anger at anti-slavery views, threats of violence, and dismissal of pastors by angry congregations, on top of legal repression. After all, slavery was blessed by the Bible and had been good for the slaves: "we see traces of an all-wise Providence in permitting the black man to be brought here and subjected to the discipline of slavery tempered by Christianity and regulated by law," concluded a historian of Virginia's colonization efforts. Anti-slavery feelings in the churches waxed cold.

Over the next decade, the main churches, Methodist, Baptist and Presbyterian, retreated from anti-slavery views, as did the smaller ones, the Christians, Cumberland Presbyterians, and Moravians; slavery was upheld by the Bible, they concluded, and they condemned the abolitionists. Kentucky, for example: "After 1830 some anti-slavery activity continued to be displayed in local churches or conferences in Kentucky, but it soon showed signs of decadence and by 1840 it had almost entirely disappeared." The exceptions here are the stalwart, permanent anti-slavery Quakers and the breakaway Wesleyan Methodists of the 1840's. A preacher in Georgia later wrote: "Proslaveryism had become the prevailing sentiment in both Church and state." The religious revival stalled. The Northern abolitionists were to blame. "It cannot be denied that the Northern movements did sensibly affect the feeling in favor of the religious instruction of the negroes throughout the whole slaveholding states, and the first prominent cause of the decline in the revival of which we speak was unquestionably those movements."

IV. Fear of Insurrection Haunts the South after 1830

A. A Plot for Slave Insurrection Is Discovered in Camden, South Carolina in 1816

In 1816, a plot of insurrection by slaves in Camden, South Carolina, was foiled when a slave told his master of the plot. The insurrection had been planned to take place on July 4th. The City Council and the Governor marshaled evidence, arrested the plotters, and tried them; six were hanged and one imprisoned. One of the members of the City Council wrote in a newspaper that, "[i]t is melancholy to reflect that those who were most active in the Conspiracy occupied a respectable stand in one of the churches, several were [Christians] and one a [Bible] class leader." The rapid response of the authorities to the plot, including the trials, was intended to calm the fears of the whites and provided a template for the response to the Vesey plot six years later.

B. The Vesey Plot Is Discovered in Charleston, South Carolina in 1822

The plan, led by Denmark Vesey, was to organize the slaves, and, on June 16, 1822, seize arsenals, attack guardhouses, attack whites, burn down parts of Charleston, seize ships and sail to Haiti. Vesey was a free black man and had been born a slave in Haiti, where he lived until a teen. As a teen, he was bought by a sea captain from Charleston and served the sea captain well for twenty years. Then, Vesey won a lottery prize of $1500, purchased his freedom and worked as a carpenter. Vesey could read and write and was a preacher; visions led him to lead the plot. Vesey's key slave-helper in the plot was later described: "He reads and writes with great and equal facility, and obviously seems to have been the individual who held the pen at all the meetings; at which he wrote more than one letter" to contacts in the Caribbean. Another key helper was described as "[b]orn a conjurer and a physician, in his own country [of Angola]" who secretly continued to do both as a slave in South Carolina for fifteen years, all the while making "charms and amulets." This key slave-helper met with others on a farm and prepared cartridges and pikes there because the overseer was black and "because the farm was accessible by water, thus enabling them to elude the patrol." Yet another slave-helper of Vesey was a saddle-maker who could read and write; he wrote a letter to Haiti's president seeking help in the plot. Another slave-helper of Vesey was a Bible class leader of the African church.

Vesey was described this way in a confession by one of the slaves: "He was in the habit of reading to me all the passages in the newspapers that related to [Haiti], and apparently every pamphlet he could lay his hands on, that had any connexion with slavery. He one day brought me a speech which he told me had been delivered in Congress by a Mr. King on the subject of slavery."

Rebel meetings were held at Vesey's house. The rebels made 250 pike heads and bayonets and over 300 daggers. The rebels stole a keg of gunpowder and were prepared to make cartridges for guns. The leaders had guns and swords. The slaves were told that the whites planned to slaughter the blacks. A month ahead of time, one of the leaders told his owner of the plot. Then, "[s]ixteen hundred rounds of ball cartridges were provided" to the city guard, "and the sentinels and patrols ordered on duty with loaded arms. Such had been our fancied security, that the guard had previously gone on duty without muskets, with sheathed bayonets and bludgeons," wrote the Charleston City Council in its post-rebellion report. There were, within weeks, 131 arrests and 67 convictions. Of those convicted, 32 were deported and 35 were executed, including Vesey. Of the 35 executed, 34 were slaves.

The failed Vesey plot of 1822, organized in Charleston, was notable in that its adherents were mostly city-folk, with city jobs, called "mechanics" at the time. Mechanics were carpenters, saddle-makers, tailors and cap makers, mill workers and blacksmiths, boatmen and pilots, along with workers on the ports or on the railroads. A newspaper in South Carolina in 1822 published an article that reflected the fear of slaves with skills. "The great fundamental principle should be that the slave should be kept as much as possible to agricultural labors. These so employed are found to be the most orderly and obedient of slaves. There should be no black mechanics or artisans, at least in the cities."

The African Methodist Episcopal Church (AME) had been formed in Northern cities in 1816;

the blacks of Charleston went, for a season, to their own black church - 3,000 strong - until the Vesey plot was discovered. Then the Charleston City Council reported that "a decided majority of the Insurgents, either did or had belonged to the African Congregation, amongst whom the inlistments principally and successfully carried on." The city closed the church "on the ground that it tended to spread the dangerous infection of the alphabet." The City Marshal told "ministers of the gospel and others who keep night and Sunday schools for slaves, that the education of such persons is forbidden by law, and that the city government feel imperiously bound to enforce the penalty." After the Vesey plot, the pastor of the AME church in Charleston was forced to move to Philadelphia, the blacks of the Charleston "returned to white congregations," and "the city government demolished the church building."

Soon, in Williamsburg, Virginia, the African Baptist Church was closed; in other towns, slaveowners switched the slaves to white churches. Elsewhere, blacks were barred from white churches. The vibe of the now-white churches suffered: without blacks in the back gallery, wrote a white Charlestonian, the "absence of their responses and hearty songs were really felt to be a loss to those so long accustomed to hear them."

Yet, the Baptists, especially, still attracted black members, ordained black preachers and opened or widened black churches. The earliest black Baptist churches were in Virginia and Georgia; they grew, too, in Kentucky, Alabama, Mississippi and Louisiana. These were mainly town churches, drawing from the towns and the countryside. Black churches grew the easiest in the 'border states' of Kentucky, Missouri, Tennessee, and, for the Methodists, in Baltimore, Maryland. Other than the Baptists, it was only the Methodists that regularly ordained black preachers, but the Methodists founded few black churches, though they were the leaders of both the post-1830 plantation mission movement and the post-1830 camp meeting movement. Black ministers were scarce or non-existent among the Presbyterians, Lutherans, Episcopalians and Moravians.

After the Vesey plot, many repressive laws were passed and actions taken: for example, Charleston banned slaves from entering the city on Sundays and a volunteer military group was formed there. The free blacks and slaves got the message; with the passage of years under the new legal regime, it could be said that "the death of Denmark Vesey and Nat Turner proved long since to the Negro the present hopelessness of physical defence." The Vesey plot was a plot that was never executed; the Nat Turner rebellion of 1831 covered a small area, perhaps 3,000 acres, of Virginia; the plot was also destroyed in mere days. Yet, the reaction was as if the slaves of all of the South had risen up in unison and been defeated. The improbable Vesey and Nat Turner conspiracies became the chief public excuses for a regime of enhanced legal snares and nets that encompassed the daily life of millions of blacks. Twenty-five years after Nat Turner's rebellion, Frederick Douglas wrote that the slave's "right to revolt is perfect," yet it is hard to find such sentiments elsewhere before the Civil War.

Charleston, at the time of the Vesey plot, had been a river city with key Atlantic ports for the prior two centuries, and was a city where slaves outnumbered whites; in the Beaufort District, for example, there were 27,339 slaves and 4,679 whites. Charleston was also home to large slave marts; in addition; eight percent of the black population was free. The white citizens of Charleston wrote a letter to their representatives in state government soon after the discovery of the Vesey plot. They proposed that all free blacks be deported, and, in the meantime, banned from owning land. Free blacks, the letter said, place "temptations" and "conditions before the eyes of the slaves which they cannot peaceably realize" and were responsible for "the dissemination of dangerous ideas and news items which the slaves would not otherwise learn." The new laws were made so "that we may extinguish at once every gleam of hope which the slaves may indulge of ever becoming free - and that we may proceed to govern them on the only principle that can maintain slavery, the 'principle of fear.'"

The letter proposed banning the hiring out of slaves, banning them from living together without a white present and banning their importation from other states. The death penalty for whites who abetted a slave plot was called for. A dress code for slaves was suggested allowing them to wear only "coarse woolens" or "coarse cotton stuffs," so that "every distinction should be created between the whites and the negroes, calculated to make the latter feel the superiority of the former." The citizens also proposed replacing the city guard with a full-time police force. "And we recommend that a law be passed, prohibiting under severe penalties, all persons from teaching negroes to read and write."

Meanwhile, a new state law jailed free blacks whose ships were in port in Charleston. Free black men, under yet another new state law, were required to have a white guardian, and to get and carry a certificate from the local court signed by the guardian.

The year after the Vesey plot of 1822, South Carolina made it a crime to bring a free black into the state who had ever been on free soil, or around it; the law banned free blacks who had ever been to the North, to the Caribbean, or to Mexico. Charleston built guardhouses and established the Citadel, an outgrowth of the city's police, which became a military school. "The gentry began to organize extralegal vigilante groups like the South Carolina Association to enforce laws against blacks." In 1837, a visitor wrote:

> Charleston keeps in pay a company of police soldiers, who during the night occupy several posts. They have their guard house near Jones's Hotel, and I was startled to hear the retreat and reveille beat there. This corps owes its support to the fear of the negroes. At

nine o'clock in the evening a bell is
sounded; and after this no negro can
venture without a written permission
from his master, or he will immediately
be thrown into prison, nor can his owner
obtain his release till next day, by the
payment of a fine. Should the master
refuse to pay this fine, then the slave
receives twenty-five lashes.

C. The Reaction to Nat Turner's 1831 Slave Rebellion

Nat Turner's rebellion has been described this
way: "The Southampton insurrection is the only
recorded instance in the South of a servile
insurrection deserving the name." In the days
following Turner's rebellion, there was agitation
among slaves and whites throughout the South.
Militias were called up all over; patrols called to duty.
In Virginia itself, "[s]ome prisoners taken near Cross
Keys were shot by the Murfreesboro troops and their
heads were left for weeks stuck up on poles as a
warning to all who should undertake a similar plot.
The captain of the marines, as they marched through
Vicksville, on their way home, bore upon his sword
the head of a rebel." The word "lynching" entered the

language of the press. A newspaper said, in 1835, "[a]nd in the south we almost daily hear of 'judge Lynch,' and of persons who are flogged and driven away, or 'executed,' under sentences rendered by him.'" Abolitionists were silenced by violence in the South for a season; the word "lynching" did not always mean murder, at the time. "In the slave States such punishment was generally a whipping or flogging, often followed by tarring and feathering, inflicted upon abolitionists or any persons suspected of 'tampering with the slaves,' or distributing 'incendiary tracts.'"

Lynch law against slaves and abolitionists continued until the Civil War; by then, perhaps 300 abolitionists had been murdered by vigilantes in the South. On the eve of the War a young Texan wrote a letter to a friend in Connecticut.

> I solemnly declare that to-day the negro
> is not as free as he was two or five years
> ago; and why? Simply because his
> master has been goaded on to
> desperation by incendiary acts and
> speeches. Now he fears the negro, and
> binds him down as you would a savage

animal. One year ago, all was peace and quietness here. The negro was allowed to go out, to have dances and frolics; to-day one dare not show his head after nine o'clock in the evening. Seven companies of patrols are organized and guard the city each night, sixteen horse-patrol scour the country around. Forty-eight vigilance men say live, banish or die, as the proof may go to show. And so it is all over the country. Men are hung every day by the decision of planters, lawyers, judges and ministers. It is no hot impetuous act, but cool, stern justice. It is the saving of wife and daughter, mother and sister from the hand of desecration.

D. White Fear after the Nat Turner Insurrection

The fear of Nat Turner-type insurrections spread after 1831 and stayed throughout the South. It was said of Virginia that after 1831, "[e]very August the alarm was given and the people rushed headlong to the swamps, the negroes as well as the whites, each household trusting the fidelity of its own, but suspecting that of the other slaves of the neighborhood." Slave plots, white alarms, vigilante committees, and hangings occurred on a widespread basis again in 1835; this season of terror was marked in Georgia, South Carolina, North Carolina, Virginia, Maryland, Alabama, Louisiana and Texas. Ideas for new laws were rampant. "Petitions were presented that slaves and free negroes be forbidden to own hogs, dogs, and other property, and that they be denied the privilege of becoming millers, mechanics, tradesmen, etc. These requests were rejected as being unnecessary and unbecoming."

Virginia's Colonization Society stepped up its work; it sent free blacks to Liberia and Ohio until the Civil War. Its former governor said, a decade later, of the Liberian operation, "Africa gave to Virginia a savage and a slave; Virginia gives back to Africa a citizen and a Christian." Perhaps many of the 3,700 free blacks who left Virginia for Liberia over the years left willingly; many did not though all were thought to have been "converted" to the idea of colonization. An anti-slavery Virginian argued in the state chambers, "[a] lynch club - a committee of vigilance - could easily exercise a kind of inquisitorial surveillance over any neighborhood, and convert any desired number, I have no doubt, at any time, into a willingness to be removed."

The fear began early. Just weeks after the Turner rebellion of 1831 in Southampton, Virginia, one of George Washington's nieces wrote a letter to Boston: "it is like a smothered volcano, we know not when, or where, the flame will burst forth but we know that death in the most horrid forms threaten us. Some have died, others have become deranged from apprehension since the South Hampton affair."

A Virginia planter wrote to Ohio:

> These insurrections have alarmed my wife so as really to endanger her health, and I have not slept without anxiety in three months. Our nights are sometimes spent in listening to noises. A corn song, or a hog call, has often been the subject of nervous terror, and a cat, in the dining room, will banish sleep for the night. There has been and there still is a panic in all this country. I am beginning to lose my courage about the melioration of the South. Our revivals produce no preachers;

churches are like the buildings in which they worship, gone in a few years. There is no principle of life. Death is an autocrat of the slave regions.

A Virginia newspaper wrote: "[W]e hear a report of a Patrol going upon an estate in Prince George and upon the overseer's pointing out five whom he suspect, shooting two who were attempting to escape, and securing the other three and throwing them into jail." North Carolina's white fear was intense; Nat Turner's insurrection took place on North Carolina's doorstep, and similar plots were suspected in neighboring counties. "Even Raleigh was put into a state of defense, even the old men past the militia age volunteering for service."

The reaction in North Carolina was swift.

In 1831-32, North Carolina passed a law forbidding free blacks to "teach or preach" at any prayer meeting, under penalty of 39 lashes; the law was passed at a secret session of the lawmakers. It later became a crime to teach slaves to read; that law was opposed by the Quakers. Free blacks, who had been able to vote since 1776, lost the right to vote. "The patrol was now given large powers of arrest. The patrollers were enjoined to visit suspected places, to disperse dangerous assemblages of slaves, to be diligent in arresting runaways, to detect thefts, and to report persons who traded with slaves." And: "If a negro who was being whipped was insolent to them he might be further punished not to exceed thirty-nine lashes in all," a survey of North Carolina law said. The Quakers, always a friend to the slave in North Carolina, and early and stubborn abolitionists, were forced to hold their last meeting in Greensboro of their Manumission Society in 1834; just seven years earlier, it had forty branches in the state.

It might be dangerous to pray in the wake of Nat Turner's rebellion. A former slave, Charity Bowery, recalled: "The brightest and best men were killed in Nat's time. Such ones are always suspected. All the colored folks were afraid to pray, in the time of the Old Prophet Nat."

There were strong feelings against Yankees and free black preachers among the politicians. The governor of Virginia wrote a letter in 1831 to the governor of South Carolina. In it, he states that "the spirit of insubordination which has, and still manifests itself in Virginia, had its origin among, and emanated from, the Yankee population, upon their first arrival amongst us, but mostly especially the Yankee peddlers and traders." The letter continued, "principally Northern" preachers told the slaves of equality, and "religion became, and is, the fashion of the times - finally our females and of the most respectable were persuaded that it was piety to teach negroes to read and write, to the end that they might read the Scriptures - many of them became tutoresses in Sunday schools and, pious distributors of tracts, from the New York Tract Society." The Virginia governor wrote that "large assemblages of negroes were suffered to take place for religious purposes. Then commenced the efforts of the black preachers, often from the pulpits these pamphlets and papers were read - followed by the incendiary publications of Walker, Garrison and Knapp of Boston, these too with songs and hymns of a similar character were circulated, read and commented upon. We rested in apathetic security until the Southampton affair." The letter also noted: "I am fully convinced that every black preacher in the whole country east of the Blue Ridge was in [on] the secret."

Twenty years after Nat Turner the white fear of black insurrection was still white hot. A Georgia planter spoke to a newspaper editor in 1850 about the abolitionists and the problems they created for a planter like himself. "[A]bolitionism," the planter said, "is even now kindling a blaze under his dwelling and Negro cabins, and he is thereby rendered so miserable that he cannot sleep soundly at nights for fear of waking up some fine morning without a single 'wooly head' he can call his own!"

V. The Churches Propose Oral Instruction of the Slaves

The tightening of laws about patrols and black religion was part of the reaction; another part was the view from the perspective of the white churches. An Episcopal member of the clergy from South Carolina expounded on the idea that blacks were descendants of the biblically-cursed Ham. As such, blacks were destined to "the lowest state of servitude, slaves." A Virginia newspaper followed up on this argument, writing that "the present condition of the African is inevitable; all efforts to extinguish black slavery are idle." The Southern churches eased any tension between their religious beliefs and slavery by becoming allies of the slaveholders, both in theology and in the fields of red earth. It then became the goal of the main Southern churches to buttress slavery by Christianizing the slaves under the approving nods of the largest slaveholders. As a black preacher said at the time, "if you give us the Gospel it will do more for the obedience of servants and the peace of the community than all your guards, guns and bayonets."

A. The Idea of Teaching Religion to the Slaves Is Driven by Northern Criticism

Religious instruction of slaves was driven by Northern criticism. An abolitionist writer who attacked the lack of religion taught to the slaves was Pastor Leonard Bacon of Connecticut. He agreed, as did so many of his Northern peers in the growing abolitionist movement, that slaves "were kept in heathenish darkness, by laws expressly enacted to make their instruction a criminal offense." This common argument by abolitionists made the Southern churches determined to prove it wrong by teaching the slaves a light version of Christianity. The light version of Christianity accepted slavery as biblically sound, biblically inevitable and an overall good thing for the slaves, taught slaves to obey, and crucially avoided teaching - as an open strategy - the slaves to read or write.

An Englishwoman named Francis Kemble opposed slavery, privately, in letters to American friends before the Civil War, and collected, in a book, the letters and her reminiscences after the War. She was the wife of the owner of one of the plantations that she visited. She stayed on a cotton and rice plantation on a Georgian swamp island for a year; her book covered that year. She wrote of teaching religion to slaves in the 1830's: "The process is a very ticklish one, and but for the Northern public opinion, which is now pressing the slaveholders close, I dare say would not be attempted at all." And: "Until the late abolition movement, the spiritual interests of the slaves were about as little regarded as their physical necessities." The slaveowners were simply set upon a "plan of making Christians of their cattle." The slaves left the island by rowboat for the town once a week, and went to services once a month, with a white preacher: "There were a short time ago two free black preachers in this neighborhood, but they have lately been ejected from the place."

The "ticklish process" of giving religious instruction to the slaves after 1830 was motivated by abolition's argument that the vast bulk of slaves were not Christian, and should have been converted decades, even centuries, earlier. The goal of religion thereafter became simpler in the South, as an Episcopalian pamphlet from South Carolina said. The goal was "to show from the Scriptures of the Old and New Testament, that slavery is not forbidden by the Divine Law: and at the same time to prove the necessity of giving religious instruction to our Negroes." The plantation mission movement took firm hold in the early 1830's; its base was ground zero of large-scale gang labor: the swamps and coasts of Georgia and South Carolina, the cotton and rice plantations of the lowlands, and on through the dark clay hills of Alabama and the plains, prairies, river lowlands, and pine woods of central Mississippi. For it was the large, and rapidly growing, plantations that saw the traveling white missionary.

If it was true that white preachers could help the slaveowners keep the slaves in check, it was also true that black preachers, rare as they were, were a danger on a large plantation. The gospel, it was said by a scholar of the time, was "the best instrument to preserve peace and good conduct among the negroes," if preached by trusted whites. The Methodists abandoned anti-slavery views and took the position that the gospel could not be read as "breathing hostility to any civil institution." Owners of large plantations came "to the knowledge of this change in the dispositions of the Methodist preachers" and consented to the missions to the slaves. But black preachers could not be trusted in fields of gang labor. It was said that:

> [O]n the large plantations of the seaboard country in South Carolina and Georgia, where the only white persons were the overseer and his family, it was quite another matter. Who could assure the owner that under the pretense of preaching the gospel to his negroes the itinerant preacher, a stranger oftentimes, would not instill principles of rebellion in the minds of the slaves?

B. The Churches Retreat from Opposition to Slavery and Propose, to the Slaveholders, That the Slaves Be Taught Christian Ideas Orally

Thus, the mainline churches by the mid-1830's sought to teach religion - orally - to the slaves, and to encourage slaveowners to do so, within the accepted, state-sponsored boundary of never teaching the slaves the read the alphabet or to write their name. For example, the pro-slavery, white scholar and pastor, Charles Jones, delivered a sermon, published in the newspapers, in 1831, before planters in Georgia called

"The Religious Instruction of the Negroes"; the local planters themselves had organized to promote religious instruction of the slaves. The address says that it "refers exclusively to Plantation Negroes." The address argued that the slaves "are men," and so it was the duty of "our country" to preach the gospel to them, even though slaves "naturally hate the light." That duty had been neglected. It is proper that the duty to teach religious ideas to the slaves falls "on us, their legal owners; for they are wholly at our disposal." The slaves needed the gospel, for "they appear to us to be without Hope and without God in the world" and full of "vice," and, on Sundays, spent "a day of idleness and sleep, of sinful amusements, of visiting, or of labor." One vice of the slaves, theft, noted Pastor Jones, was worthy of this example: "Their depredations of rice have been estimated to amount to twenty-five percent on the gross average of crops." He did not mention the hunger of the slaves.

The slaveowners and the churches had the legal power to instruct the slaves, for the "civil law does not forbid us to give them the Gospel orally"; moreover, such instruction did not violate any slaveowner's "property or liberty." Many slaves "never go to church at all," and, "only a part can go on each Sabbath, as it is not permitted" or "desirable." The "majority do not hear the Gospel for weeks and months altogether." During the week, only a few plantations gave religious instruction.

The new method of instruction, argued Pastor Jones, should include missionaries - only "Southern men." "[T[he Negroes for the most part must be instructed at night," and so the wide extent of the territory allowed only visits to the "plantations in rotation." Setting up small churches - "stations"- near the plantations would fail because "[o]nly a part of every plantation is allowed to be away at any one time." The best plan: "The Planters form themselves into a voluntary association, and take the religious instruction of the colored population into their own hands." That instruction would be done "altogether orally." The teachers would be the planters or those locals - "the teacher will not ride . . . more than a few miles" - appointed by them. The teachers "are to confine themselves to the religious instruction of the Negroes wholly; nor are they to intermeddle with the concerns of the plantation in any manner, nor repeat abroad what their eyes hear, or their eyes see on them." Finding such teachers will be hard; "the white population is so sparse and so few of them, if any, are pious." The style of teaching, Pastor Jones said later in his book, must be controlled. No audible expressions of feeling in the way of groanings, cries, or noises of any kind, should be allowed. "To encourage such things among ignorant people, such as they are, would be to jeopardize the interests of true religion, and open the door to downright fanaticism."

The benefits, argued Pastor Jones, were that the slaves will learn "their duties towards us," including the duty to obey, and the authority of the masters "will be strengthened." Pastor Jones cited another pastor, who had written of the slaves that "a sense of duty would counteract their reluctance to labor, and diminishing the cases of feigned sickness, so harrassing to the planter." "Their work," as Pastor Jones wrote in his 300-page book on the subject, "would be more faithfully done; their obedience more universal and more cheerfully rendered."

A major benefit, too, Pastor Jones said in his sermon, would be that the effect of the "Patrol Laws" would be enhanced: "For the simple presence of a white man at stated times amongst the Negroes, will tend greatly to the promotion of good order." The white instructors, Pastor Jones also wrote, will "exert a restraining influence upon any spirit of insubordination that may exist, and at the same time give opportunities for its detection." His book pointed out that placing white instructors among the slaves would prevent "the danger of leaving them to the control of their own ignorant, fanatical and designing preachers," such as Vesey and Turner themselves or those heading the recently formed African Methodist churches.

Indeed, the sermon continued, the Vesey rebellion in Charleston in 1822 would have been prevented "[i]f our plan of sending a white instructor into every assembly of Negroes for religious purposes had been in operation." After all, the Moravian slaves in Jamaica during the mass rising of slaves against their British owners, that very year, ending in the deaths of 200 slaves, 14 whites, and resulting in the execution of 312 slaves, "had, to a man, supported the authority of their Masters against the insurgents." Another benefit: "a faithful Servant is more profitable than an unfaithful one." Another benefit: white morals would improve, since, without the instruction, "the influence of the Negroes on the morals of our white population, is exceedingly pernicious."

C. The Camp Meeting Movement, a White Revival, Takes off after 1830

The camp meetings, emerging with strength in the 1830's, were not part of the plantation; the plantations, instead, got short visits from missionaries. A Methodist missionary in South Carolina wrote, "[w]e had no protracted meetings on negro missions. Our preaching was confined chiefly to the Sabbath. Revivals, as conducted among the whites, were not practicable."

At the same time, in stark contrast, a feverous religious revival - a white one - gripped the South, and separation from national churches took hold. The Methodist revival of 1826-27 spread from Virginia to Georgia and then westward. Camp meetings of all denominations - Methodist, Baptist and Presbyterian - drew 5,000, mixing planters, poor white and black folks and slaves; a Jackson, Tennessee meeting drew 20,000.

Religious and political fanaticism shared the same stage and Bible. "By the 1820's, southern Baptists and Methodists were denying that slavery constituted a 'question of morals at all.'" A meeting in 1835 in Mississippi passed a resolution that slavery was "not felt as an evil, moral or political, but . . . a blessing both to master and slave."

The gatherings grew. "By the 1840's camp meetings were annual affairs, lasting a few days to two weeks or more." And through it all: "From Virginia to Texas, revivals prepared the South to meet the abolitionist offensive." The awakenings led to a Southern church that became officially in-line with the slaveholders: arguments over slavery led to an historic secession of Southern churches - the Methodist Episcopal Church, South formed in 1844. Thus, the traveling Methodist missionaries to the large slave plantations became even more trusted by the slaveowners, for, with their new Southern church, "[t]here was no longer any danger that the professed missionary would become an incendiary."

A Swedish writer named Fredrika Bremer spent a couple of years traveling in the United States; she spent months in South Carolina and Georgia in 1849. She evidently planned to write a novel, and, during her travels, she wrote long, detailed letters of her observations to her mother and sister back in Sweden. Bremer did not write the novel, but published the letters instead. Bremer attended a camp meeting in Georgia of three or four thousand people; two-thirds were slaves. It was held in a clearing in the woods, and the people met under a long, long wooden roof held up by beams, with a stage in the center and a pulpit upon the stage. There were "four preachers, who, during the intervals between the hymns, addressed the people with loud voices, calling sinners to conversion and amendment of life." The hymns of the slaves in many of their tents were sung all night long. A common sight was to see "a rocking movement of women, who held each other by the hand in a circle, singing the while" - a mournful lamentation refined in the furnace of affliction.

Yet, when blacks attended camp meetings with whites, they were taken for a happy economic class. A Mississippi pastor and head of a college, in 1841, wrote a book against the abolitionists. The slaves "are, we believe, the happiest labouring class, as they exist and are situated in Maryland, Virginia and the South, of any in the world." And:

> Who that ever saw the thousands of
> negroes collected at a camp meeting,
> from the Eastern and Western Shores
> of Maryland and Virginia, on the

Tangier Islands in the Chesapeake Bay, or at those meetings in the South, thousands of thousands, in Georgia and the Carolinas, will not say so? Singing, praying, preaching, day and night, free as air. 'How can they sing,' say abolitionists? How can they sing, ask you sirs? Why for the very best of reasons. They want but little.

The slaves, wrote the Mississippi pastor, were "a race once savage," but Southern slavery had made them into "an enlightened and religious people" and "as a labouring class one of the happiest in all the world."

The Baptists of Kentucky, for example, joined the camp meeting movement in the late 1830's and a Baptist revival - 30,000 Kentuckians were baptized - took hold in Kentucky from 1837 to 1843. The Baptists had, in prior years, largely rejected what they called "schemes" of any kind for worship, and so had been against "missions, Sunday-schools, Bible societies, Colleges, Protracted Meetings and 'larned' preachers." Once Kentucky's Baptists started having long camp meetings, annual revivals became common, and the church grew, divided at first among missionary and non-missionary, occasional, house-church branches. In a 'border state' like Kentucky, the steady acts of the Underground Railroad after 1840 riled the slaveowners. The founding of the abolitionist newspaper called *The True American* in 1843 in Lexington by Cassius Clay agitated the Bluegrass region. Then, "sixty prominent citizens" took possession "of *The True American* press, type, and printing apparatus" and sent it all to Cincinnati. Later, the Baptists of Kentucky, like those in all of the Southern slave states, severed from their Northern brethren in 1845 and formed the Southern Baptist Convention.

White or black, the camp meetings were not all godly. A white memory: "[T]here is much whiskey sold at these gatherings, and the people drink and play at cards while others attend to religion." Also, the effects of a revival might not last that long. After a revival, wrote a Methodist minister, "[m]any remain in the church only a few months, or at most but one or two years."

D. The Missionary Movement to the Slaves of the Plantations Takes off after 1830

The missionary movement was real enough, but was it widespread at the time? Looking back, the missionary movement is connected to the spectacular growth of black churches in the South after the Civil War. Before that, caution about numbers is called for. The highly respected scholar Albert J. Raboteau, author of the 1978 masterwork, *Slave Religion: The 'Invisible Institution' in the Antebellum South*, made a powerful point that suggests caution in describing the extent of Christian slaves in the South before the War. "The majority of slaves," he wrote, "remained only minimally touched by Christianity by the second decade of the nineteenth century." This point underscores how powerfully Christianity caught on between 1820-1861 among slaves. W.E.B. DuBois wrote that, in 1859, there were 468,000 black church members in the South, but that number would grow to an astounding 2.7 million church members within forty years.

The Presbyterian Synod of South Carolina and Georgia said as late as 1833 that, across Maryland and South Carolina, there were "not twelve men exclusively devoted to the religious instruction of the Negroes." The report continued:

But do not the Negroes have access to the gospel through the stated ministry of the whites? We answer, no. The Negroes have no regular and efficient ministry: as a matter of course, no churches; neither is there sufficient room in the white churches for their accommodation. We know of but five churches in the slaveholding states, built expressly for their use. These are all in the state of Georgia. We may now inquire whether they enjoy the privileges of the gospel in their own homes? Again we return a negative answer. They have no Bibles to read by their own firesides. They have no family altars; and when in affliction, sickness or death, they have no minister to address to them the consolations of the gospel, nor to bury them with appropriate services.

The next year a report said: "If the master is pious, the house servants alone attend family worship, and frequently few or none of them, while the field hands have no attention at all."

Of the plantation missions, the Southern Methodists took the lead, while Baptists, Presbyterians and Episcopalians worked on conversions. The post-1830 mission movement was christened the "Mission to Slaves." The effect, in raw numbers, of the mission movement was not dramatic, in the short run: 1242 converted adult slaves in all of Georgia and South Carolina by 1831, with an increase of only 165 that year. Yet, in 1834 one preacher alone at the New River mission "wrote of preaching in a barn and under a stand in the woods to congregations of negroes that averaged not less than 800 to 1,000 each time."

A well-known sermon in South Carolina in 1832 described the goals of the Mission to Slaves. "He pointed to the converted negro (the noblest prize of the gospel) the most unanswerable proof of its efficiency. There he was, mingling his morning song with the matin-chorus of the birds, sending up his orisons to God under the light of the evening star, contented with his lot, cheerful in his labors, submissive for conscience sake to plantation discipline."

The pro-slavery impulse of the mission movement was obvious to all. "[T]he Mission to Slaves was developed to combat African heathenism, foil abolitionism, and continue the earliest commitments made to blacks during the early antislavery impulse." In Tennessee, "[a]nti-slavery workers from all denominations left the state" during this time, and "manumission societies died." The "owners of large plantations" in Tennessee now, for the first time, gave their "consent to permit their slaves to hear the gospel from the lips of capable white missionaries."

And it was true that, after 1830, the white churches got busy. W.E.B. DuBois wrote that "[a] minister in Mississippi testified that he had charge of the Negroes of five plantations and three hundred slaves; another in Georgia visited eighteen plantations every two weeks." A Methodist missionary in South Carolina in 1835 wrote a letter about his work. His mission, he wrote, "embraces 11 plantations, which are visited every week - children divided into 11 classes, which I instruct orally. By the aid of [two other missionaries] Divine service is held on from 4 to 6 plantations every Sunday. We have 310 members that continue to evince their desire of salvation." Many large slaveowners began to support the missions to the slaves after 1830; a missionary in the swamps of the Savannah River wrote that in December, 1834, "forty-four planters desired their slaves should be taken into the mission. [. . .] The planters built several churches, asked for two additional missionaries, and contributed over $800 to the missionary society."

The teaching of slave children in religious matters could be extensive. One mission in Georgia had "a class of nearly two hundred children under catechetical instruction." Another, the Savannah River mission, had "six schools in which 214 children were regularly catechised." On five islands below Savannah, there was "a population of 80 whites and over 1,200 blacks. There were 180 colored children in classes."

A white South Carolina preacher named George Moore was sent to the Georgia coast, its islands, its rice swamps, and mainland. Here are some of his recollections. What were the crowds like? "Our average attendance at each place is from 100 to 150," George Moore wrote.

> I went regularly round, week day and
> Sunday. We preached on Paris Island
> on Sunday, the negroes from all the

plantations attending. We had no church building at that time, but occupied a house on the plantation of our patron, Mr. Robert Means. We would also preach at some of the other places at night. I recollect on one occasion preaching with a negro holding a lightwood. At first we preached at two or three places on the island on Sunday, as we confined our labors a good deal to plantation preaching.

On a riverbank: "I generally preached in an old cooper shop opposite the Bluff Place, where the negroes from all the other plantations attended. Here we usually held a sunrise prayer meeting and catechised the children from the estate place."

On an island owned by the Sams brothers:

At the different places on Dathan we preached at night and catechised the children during the day. At Dr. Sams's, however, we preached on a week day, the negroes coming out of the fields to assemble at the appointed time in a large cotton house. At the close of the services the smaller negroes would remain to be catechised. At Mr. L. Sams's we preached at night and had some most attentive hearers.

On another island owned by one man: "Every time we visited his place he gave up the labor of sixty hands for half the day. On this place I baptized thirty at one time, twenty-nine by immersion and one, the driver, by pouring."

George Moore preached wherever he could. "At Bonnoe's Ferry I preach at Dr. Prioleau's, sometimes in a negro house and sometimes under a widespreading oak. I also preached under an old brick shed, where the negroes from several of the plantations on the eastern branch of the Cooper attend. We hope soon to have a church here."

How did George Moore travel? "In going to and fro on my work on the mission, I have ridden horseback, in a gig, and often on a negro's back. Sometimes it would be in a boat pushed through the mud. Often I have had to be pushed some distance through the mud to get to water to baptize the negroes."

Charles Wilson, a Methodist preacher in South Carolina for 22 years, recalled, "I have on some occasions preached five sermons and rode on horseback forty-five miles all in a day, leaving home at 4 o'clock in the morning and returning at 8 in the evening, sometimes much later."

It was slow going for the white missions to the slaves in the countryside, in the sugar cane fields and in the rice swamps: "The turbulent slaveholders who conquered the Old Southwest in the 1820's and 1830's came to religion slowly and could hardly have been expected to try to bring their slaves on any faster." The fact remained that, in the 1830's South, "[i]f the slaves were going to get religion, then religion had to be made safe for slaveholders." The Methodists appointed a South Carolina missionary to work with slaves in 1838. He was asked to go away, in writing, by a committee set up by 353 whites. The letter upbraided him for teaching slaves how to read in 1838 - just months after his mission began. The letter said, "Verbal instruction will increase the desire of the black population to learn. We know of upwards of a dozen negroes in the neighborhood of Cambridge who can now read, some of whom are members of your societies at Mount Lebanon and New-Salem. Of course, when they see themselves encouraged, they will supply themselves with Bibles, hymn books, and Catechisms!" The growth of these tendencies, the letter said, "will ultimately revolutionize our civil institutions," for "[i]ntelligence and slavery have no affinity with each other."

The missionaries of the 1830's were often met with fear and anger from the whites. Many slaveholders, incensed by the emerging abolition-now movement in the North, attacked the Southern churches. "Persecution of those who undertook to preach to the Negroes was now rife in every direction." In the 1830's it could again be said that "[e]very Methodist preacher was regarded as an abolitionist agent," and often suffered violence as a result. After all, "on the large plantations, where the overseer and his family were the only white people, who could assure the owner that under the pretense of preaching the Gospel his Negroes would not be stirred up to rebellion?' The Methodists, when they split into a Northern branch and a slavery-supporting Southern branch in 1844, did so "to prevent the destruction of the Methodist Church in the South."

The missionary movement, nevertheless, got results. Here are raw numbers for churches in South Carolina. The Methodists said they had 42,000 black members by 1821; the Methodists could have had more black members, but had a curious, chilly attitude towards music. Wrote one British traveler of Georgia: "[o]n the Hopeton plantation above twenty violins have been silenced by the Methodist missionaries." Another visitor recalled,

> I have since heard that the Methodist missionaries, who are the most influential and effective teachers and preachers among the negroes, are very angry with them for their love of dancing and music, and declare them to be sinful. And whenever the negroes become Christian, they give up dancing, have preaching meetings instead, and employ their musical talents merely on psalms and hymns.

The Methodists of South Carolina, in 1839, reported that they had 19 missionaries in the state serving 210 plantations. Across the South, by 1840, about ten percent of the 2.4 million slaves were formally

Christian, with 80,000 Baptists, 80,000 Methodists, and several smaller churches. The Southern Baptist Convention split from its Northern brethren in 1845. Yet, the Baptists were open to black preachers and black churches, and Baptists after 1845 had the majority of black preachers and black churches in the South; most of those black churches had white preachers, but the efforts were made. The Methodists, after 1844, had black members in their churches, stations, circuits and missions, and had occasional black preachers. Most preachers of all denominations were, of course, white. This was a common slave memory: "The first time I was sprinkled a white preacher did it."

If a male slaveowner was a religious man, then "if he was a Methodist, his slaves were Methodists; if he was a Baptist, his slaves were Baptists; if he was a Presbyterian, his slaves were Presbyterians; and if he was an Episcopalian, his slaves were Episcopalians." The brilliant scholar of slavery, Eugene Genovese, wrote, however, that the slaveowners did not typically force their slaves to adopt a denomination. He noted that "a plantation had to take whatever preacher came through the area regardless of his sect." As a Methodist missionary in Mississippi recalled: "Many of the negroes on these plantations were of Baptist persuasion themselves, but their owners were either Methodists or of no Church affiliation. But there was no sectarian feeling shown in having the gospel preached to their slaves. Many who belonged to no Church themselves were foremost in their efforts to help the missionary in his work."

In Alabama, the Episcopalians had three churches in Mobile that were open to free blacks and slaves; the Church of the Good Shepherd, a separate church for free blacks and slaves, was opened in 1854. The Baptists of Mobile had established the modest Stone Street Baptist Church, home for free blacks and slaves, as early as 1806. By 1859, the slave South was home to 175,000 black Baptists. A Baptist memory by a former slave, Lundsford Lane, notes that slaves got permission to join a church in North Carolina: "After obtaining from my mistress a written permit, a thing always required in such cases, I had been baptized and received into fellowship with the Baptist denomination."

VI. The Slave States Pass Laws to Control the Expanding Slave Population and Crush Insurrectionary Ideas and Possibilities

Slaveowner attitudes towards slave literacy hardened. Tom Hawkins, a former slave in Athens, Georgia, had memories: "Dere warn't no schools whar slaves could git book larnin' in dem days. Dey warn't even 'lowed to larn to read and write. When Dr. Cannon found out dat his carriage driver had larned to read and write whilst he was takin' de doctor's chillun to and f'um school, he had dat [slave's] thumbs cut off and put another boy to doin' de drivin' in his place."

And the patrols, across the South, got more power. An English traveler wrote of his visit to Alabama. "[E]very evening at nine o'clock a great bell, or curfew, tolls in the market-place of Montgomery, after which no colored man is permitted to be abroad without a pass. This custom has, I understand, continued ever since some formidable insurrections which happened several years ago in Virginia and elsewhere." Fear of the Northern abolitionists was strong in Alabama. Its legislature wrote in 1836 of "[t]he dark, deep and malignant design of the abolitionists . . . in sending to our country their agents and incendiary pamphlets and publications, lighting up fires of discord in the bosoms of our slave population."

As the slave power grew, free blacks suffered as well. For example, Tennessee banned the entry of free blacks from other states into Tennessee in 1831. That same year, the slaves were prevented from being emancipated. Tennessee passed a law that said that any slave that was already emancipated had to be deported to Africa at the expense of the slaveowner. Free blacks, too, were not truly free at all; the patrols could nab them for not having a pass. It was written that under the "existing laws, if a 'free coloured man travels without passports, certifying his right to his liberty, he is generally apprehended, and frequently plunged (with his progeny) into slavery by the operation of the laws.'"

A.   The Laws

1) Laws Prohibiting Free Blacks and Slaves from Learning to Read or Write

In the nineteenth century, if you learned to read, you did not always learn to write. The oldest laws in the slave states prohibited anyone from teaching a slave to write; in theory, at the time, if a slave learned to read, that was okay, because someday she might read a bit of the Bible. "Reading instruction, then, unlike writing instruction, was legally permitted by all the colonies throughout the colonial period in the service of Christianity."

Discussing the Gabriel plot in 1800, Judge St. George Tucker of Virginia said: "Our sole security then consists in their ignorance of this power (doing us mischief) and their means of using it - a security which we have lately found is not to be relied on, and which, small as it is, every day diminishes. Every year adds to the number of those who can read and write; and the increase in knowledge is the principal agent in evolving the spirit we have to fear."

Savannah, Georgia sits on the high ground between the Savannah River and the sea. Savannah passed an ordinance in 1817 that fined whites convicted of teaching any "person of colour, slave or free, to read or write." Less prominent in the history books, but important in day-to-day life in the towns and cities, were local ordinances about teaching slaves to read or write. Of Savannah, a newspaper wrote in 1818, "[t]he city has passed an ordinance, by which any person that teaches any person of colour, slave or free, to read or write, or causes such persons to be so taught, is subjected to a fine . . . and every person of colour who shall keep a school to teach reading or writing is subject to a fine or to be imprisoned ten days and whipped thirty-nine lashes."

South Carolina law enhanced the penalties for teaching slaves to read - writing had long been banned - in 1834. If a free black was caught doing so, he was fined and whipped - whites faced prison. In Virginia in 1854, a woman was tried for such crimes and found guilty. The judge told her, "[y]ou are guilty of one of the vilest crimes that ever disgraced society; and the jury have found you so. You have taught a slave girl to read the Bible."

Thomas Jefferson's plantation, Monticello, has been excavated in modern times; there was found, in the slave quarters, 237 unidentified slates, 27 pencil leads, 2 pencil slates, and 18 slates for writing. If given the chance, as the slaves likely were at Monticello, the slaves would, as other slaveholders feared, learn to read and write.

Slaves taught each other to read and write in large numbers in the towns. In Natchez, Louisiana, there were

> . . . two schools taught by colored teachers. One of these was a slave woman who had taught a midnight school for a year. It was opened at eleven or twelve o'clock at night, and closed at two o'clock a.m. Milla Granson, the teacher, learned to read and write from the children of her indulgent master in her old Kentucky home. Her number of scholars was twelve at a time, and when she had taught these to read and write she dismissed them, and again took her apostolic number and brought them up to the extent of her ability, until she had graduated hundreds. A number of them

wrote their own passes and started for Canada.

Slave literacy became, more and more, a target of slaveowner ire. To "prevent the general instruction of negroes in the arts of reading and writing," was, according to the Southern Literary Messenger, "a measure of police essential to the tranquility, nay to the existence of Southern society." The harsh change in attitudes was felt by the younger generation of slaves in the 1830-1850 period. A slave on a large cotton plantation owned by 'Master K' in Georgia spoke with a visitor in 1838 about his owner's change in attitude toward reading.

> Massa K, him never favor our reading, him not like it; likely as not he lick you if he find you reading; or, if you wish to teach your children, him always say, 'Pooh! Teach 'em to read! Teach 'em to work.' [. . .] [So] we never paid much attention to it; but now it will be different; it was different in former times. The old folks of my father and mother's time could read more than we

can, and I expect the people will dare to
give some thought to it again now.

Who was responsible, said the slaveowners and
their writers and educators, for the anti-literacy laws?
Anti-literacy laws were caused by outsiders, by
abolitionists - not by the desire of slaveowners to
clamp down upon and protect their chief property as
the new labor formation in the countryside, mass gang
slavery, showed its profitability and expanded. Light,
illiterate religious instruction grew. Other repressive
laws and tactics did, too, in town and country, both
against free blacks and slaves. The slave power
reached its height and used its power openly and
notoriously. But it always blamed outsiders for its
repression of blacks. The slaveowners and their
literate supporters always claimed, in unison:

> I can tell you. It was the abolition
> agitation. If the slave is not allowed to
> read his bible, the sin rests upon the
> abolitionists; for they stand prepared
> to furnish him with a key to it, which
> would make it, not a book of hope, and
> love, and peace, but of despair, hatred
> and blood; which would convert the

reader, not into a Christian, but a demon. [. . .] Allow our slaves to read your writings, stimulating them to cut our throats! Can you believe us to be such unspeakable fools?

The state legislatures got busy. Georgia, in 1829, made it unlawful for whites, slaves and free blacks to teach a slave or a free black "to read or write, either written or printed characters." Louisiana, in 1830, made it unlawful to teach a slave "to read or write."

Other states took years to pass anti-literacy laws; Missouri passed one in 1847, in the midst of anti-abolitionist frenzy. The law made it unlawful to "keep or teach" a school "for the instruction of Negroes or mulattoes." The long tradition of Catholic education of slaves in St. Louis was broken. The new law banned schools for free blacks and made it a crime to teach reading or writing to a free black or slave.

One argument in favor of anti-literacy laws, wrote a famous pro-slavery tract written by three South Carolina educators and its governor, was that the slaves had no time for the extravagance of reading.

The tract said, "[h]e who works during the day with his hands, does not read in intervals of leisure for his amusement, or the improvement of his mind." The slaves, the tract continued, had no "chance of their elevating their rank and condition in society," so suffered no hardship. "A knowledge of reading, writing, and the elements of arithmetic, is convenient and important to the free laborer, who is the transactor of his own affairs, and the guardian of his own interests but of what use would they be to the slave?" And: "As to education, you will probably admit that slave-holders should have more leisure for mental culture than most people." Slavery, the argument went, was the "sole cause" of civilization. "It is the order of nature and of God, that the being of superior faculties and knowledge, and therefore of superior power, should control and dispose of those who are inferior." The black slaves, like the Indians, were barbarians. And the example of the Indians showed the alternative to slavery if the white man was to stay in control. "Yet if anything is certain, it is certain that there were no means by which he could possess the country, without exterminating or enslaving them."

Fear of abolitionist ideas, just as cotton slavery was getting more and more profitable, and its masters were getting more and more politically powerful both within their states and in federal politics, remained the publicly-stated driving fear behind anti-literacy laws until the Civil War broke out in 1861. A preacher in Georgia said: "Our excuse for keeping them in ignorance has been the intermeddling of abolitionists, to prevent the negroes from reading their publications, which we have usually styled 'incendiary,' which term we have been in the habit of applying to every form of argument, however mild, that was intended to show us what was immoral in our institution." This was true even in states, like Kentucky, where slavery was judged to be less harsh, and, like Florida and Maryland, there was no anti-literacy law. With respect to teaching slaves to read, the Kentucky experience was described in 1829.

> Though there is no law in Kentucky designed to prohibit the teaching of slaves, yet such is the opposition made against it by the populace, that but few Sabbath-schools for the instruction of the Africans are permitted to exist in the State. It often happens that the

benevolent teachers of Sabbath-schools find themselves, and their poor, unoffending scholars, on the sacred morning, surrounded by men armed with whips, clubs and guns, for the violent dispersion of the unhappy and innocent victims of their rage! Thus Sabbath-schools are broken up in Kentucky with a violence and cruelty that ought to shame the most unfeeling band of Algerians! Nor is such violent opposition to teaching slaves confined to the more ignorant parts of the State; it is equally manifested in the most enlightened places. A few years since in the neighborhood of Lexington, and in one of the oldest and best settlements in the State, a Sabbath-school was instituted, and taught by some very respectable gentlemen, and the prospect of doing good was exceedingly fair; but, alas! all the rising hopes of benevolence were soon blasted. One sacred morning the poor slaves assembled at the school-room with the pleasing expectation of learning to read the word of eternal life: but to their sad surprise, about sixty men soon appeared for their dispersion, armed with clubs and guns, and thus the school was dispersed never to meet again!

The heat of the anti-abolitionist sentiments of the time can be felt in the report of the Charleston City Council in 1835. Of abolitionist groups and their writings, the report said, there were "250 such Societies in thirteen States, and the weekly issue from a single Press in the City of New-York, of from 25 to 50,000 copies of these Incendiary Pamphlets and Papers, with which our Public Mail has been lately burdened." The report feared the "moral pestilence" of the abolitionists and called them "incendiaries."

Slave agitation and ensuing panic gripped the South again in 1840, especially in Washington D.C., Maryland, Virginia, North Carolina, Alabama, and, especially, Louisiana. In one parish alone in Louisiana, four hundred slaves rose up; the uprising was quelled, and twenty slaves were hung.

A year after South Carolina thickened its swarm of penalties for teaching slaves to read or write, 122 slaveowners sent a petition to the legislature complaining about the anti-literacy law. The petition stridently said: "In many places this law could not be enforced. A jury could not be made [to] see how the teaching of the scriptures, or any book strictly religious, could jeopardize any interest human or divine. [. . .] [D]oes chivalrous South Carolina quail before gangs of cowardly Africans with a Bible in their hands? Let it not be said!!" This religious view did not, however, prevail; increased repression against slaves and free blacks was the order of the day. Abolitionists were attempting "to stir up a servile war," it was widely felt, and their writings originated with "the public hostility of Northern politicians to the people of the slaveholding States."

2) Laws Banning Religious and Other Gatherings of Free Blacks and Slaves

Black churches, with congregations of slaves and free blacks, were rare but growing in the 1820's; they were soon considered "nurseries of self-government" for slaves. So, black-only religion was banned.

Virginia's law of 1819 banned any nighttime meetings of free blacks and slaves as an "unlawful assembly" along with "any school or schools for teaching them reading or writing, either in the day or night."

A Milledgeville, Georgia's town council declared:

"Item, September 13, 1831: Ordered, that the marshal and deputies use increased vigilance with regard to our black population, and particularly that they do not fail to visit every place at which there is an assembly of negroes, and in the event of religious meetings to treat them as the law directs for unlawful meetings, unless there is present at least one white person."

In 1831, Delaware passed a law that said that no congregation or meeting of free blacks in a group of twelve should be held later than midnight, without three whites present. Five whites had to sponsor a free black to preach. Florida, in 1832, banned all meetings of free blacks except for religious ones with whites present.

South Carolina's law of 1800 said: "It shall not be lawful for any number of slaves, free negroes, mulattoes, or mestizoes, even of slaves in company with white persons, to meet together and assemble for the purpose of mental instruction" at night. By 1840, the law prohibited gatherings "in a confined or secret place of meeting" at any time of the day or night for "mental instruction," whether whites were present or not, and the patrols were told, by law, to "break doors, gates or windows" if they were resisted when the patrol dispersed the meeting. The law, by 1840, also banned meetings at night for "mental instruction or religious worship," whether whites were present or not. The patrols were tightened, too: fines were imposed on white men who did not take their turn to "ride patrol," though the patrollers were given immunity from lawsuits and criminal prosecution. In 1834, free blacks were barred from teaching other free blacks "to read or write." Free blacks were barred, also in 1834, from entering the state; if one was found, the law allowed "any white person to seize and convey him" before a judge.

The town of Pendleton, South Carolina, imposed a curfew ordinance in 1835 that told the patrols to "apprehend and correct" any slave on the street after 9 p.m., "whether such slave or free person of color have a pass or not."

The corn and wheat farms of East and middle Tennessee and, especially, the cotton plantations of West Tennessee were patrolled with greater vigilance after 1830. Tennessee, in 1831, banned as a crime and punished by the patrols with 25 lashes, "all assemblages of slaves in unusual numbers, or at suspicious times and places not expressly authorized by their owners."

Mississippi, in 1831, made it unlawful for free blacks or slaves "to preach the gospel."

An Alabama law passed in 1832 made it unlawful for slaves or free blacks to "preach, exhort or harangue" another slave or free black, outside "the presence of five respectable slaveholders," unless "licensed" by a local church. The law also made it a crime to teach free blacks or slaves to read. Free blacks who wrote a "pass or free-paper" for a slave got 39 lashes and deportation. The law, too, made it a crime for five slaves to gather off of a plantation, "with or without passes or permits," unless under the watch of their owner or at a white church. Free blacks were barred from preaching outside the presence of five slaveholders. In addition, Alabama banned the further entry of free blacks into the state.

In North Carolina, free blacks and slaves were prohibited from preaching, exhorting or teaching "in any prayer meeting . . . where slaves of different families are collected together" in 1835 and abolished public schools for free blacks that year as well.

Under Virginia law, all meetings of free blacks or slaves of any kind at night were banned in 1818. In 1819, all meetings of them at "schools for teaching them reading and writing, either in the day or night," were banned. In 1829, Virginia banned all schools for slaves and free blacks, even Sunday schools. The 1831-1832 laws banned meetings of free blacks "at any school-house, church, meeting-house or other place, for teaching them reading and writing, either in the day or night." One historian wrote that the 1831-1832 laws added an anti-abolitionist ban that "prescribed very rigid punishment for persons writing or printing anything advising persons of color to rebel." The result, said that historian, was "[n]ot even Nat's confession to Mr. Gray could be sold in the South."

Maryland, in 1831, banned religious gatherings of free blacks and slaves without the leadership of a white, and the white person had to stay until the end of the meeting. Constables who did not disperse black-only religious meetings could be fined. "Any slave taken at a meeting and not belonging to the owner of the place, got a good whipping." Free blacks in the largest cities, Annapolis and Baltimore, however, "could hold their services by themselves, up to the hour of ten at night, with written leave of a white licensed preacher." Religion was targeted: "In 1845, negro camp meetings and other protracted out-door meetings were forbidden." That year, also, black-led religious meetings were banned, even in Baltimore and Annapolis, but this law was soon repealed. "Negroes were still allowed, of course, to attend regular camp meetings held by the whites. In most of the incorporated towns, free negroes wandering about the streets after certain hours of night - as, for instance, nine in winter and ten in summer - were liable, as slaves were, to be taken up and given a moderate whipping or be shut up till morning, by the constables, by virtue of local ordinances." Maryland also, in 1831, began a colonization effort to remove free blacks to Liberia. The following year, 75 free-born blacks and 69 freed blacks were sent to Africa, with their consent, with the cost borne by a special tax. Within a decade of the colonizing effort, 627 men and women had been sent to Africa from Maryland, and 25 to Haiti.

The laws of Maryland banned the entry of free blacks into the state by 1807, with little effect; the laws were tightened after Nat Turner's 1831 revolt, and the fines for employing or "harboring" a free black from outside of Maryland were increased. Free blacks from outside of the state who were caught were fined, and if they could not pay the fine, enslaved and sold at public auctions at the steps of the courthouse. "The plain policy of the State was to free itself of the black population," wrote a historian of Maryland. Maryland, in 1831, banned abolitionist writings under penalty of ten to twenty years in prison; the law was strengthened in 1845, when it became the legal duty of all whites to "inform against any free black who might be, or might have been, in possession of any such papers." A free black man in 1857 was sentenced to 10 years in prison for having a copy of *Uncle Tom's Cabin*.

It did not help the slaves of the eastern states, such as Maryland, that there was a meteor shower of exceptional brightness in 1833; since slaves were taught to fear judgment day. "In 1833, when the stars fell, all the Negroes on the plantation were terrified; they hid under beds, in barn lofts, hay and straw stacks; they thought judgment day had come."

The repression of free blacks and slaves by criminalizing literacy and black religious gatherings was complete. A classic study, written in 1919, concluded: "The Sabbath-schools in which so many colored people there had learned to read and write had by 1834 restricted their work to oral instruction. [. . .] In 1840 there were in the South only fifteen colored Sabbath-schools, with an attendance of about 1459."

3) Laws Banning Abolitionist Writings

It was in the 1830's too that the Christian churches of the North began not to just oppose slavery, but to strive for "immediate and unconditional abolition" of slavery, and supported this new position with the Bible. The churches, argued the British abolitionist Charles Olcott in his widely-published lecture in 1838, must end the "criminal silence of the clergy and their criminal acquiescence in the sin of slavery." Olcott's argument was that "[s]lavery is as great a crime against the Law of God, as murder, or any other crime." At this stage, abolition still meant "the passage of the proper Law by the rightful legislative power"; Olcott thought slavery could be eliminated in a decade. After all, all you needed to do was pass a law. "There is no difficulty in preparing a statute, completely adequate to the purpose. The British abolition act does not occupy much over a square of common newspaper print." Yet, in the United States, it would take a civil war to write the law; the law is called the Thirteenth Amendment, which bans slavery.

In the towns, the slaveholder fear was that free blacks and slaves would get ahold of the new abolition-now writings from the North. Of those, there were strong tracts written by free blacks, such as David Walker's *Appeal to the Coloured Citizens of the World*, printed in Boston in 1829. "Sixty of his pamphlets found their way into Savannah, Georgia, where the mayor wrote an angry letter to the mayor of Boston to ask him to stop them; others reached New Orleans; Richmond, Virginia; and at least five cities in North Carolina." The other pamphlet by a free black man that was especially detested by the slaveholders was Robert Alexander Young's tract of 1829, *The Ethiopian Manifesto, Issued in Defence of the Black Man's Rights in the Scale of Universal Freedom.*

Laws banning abolition writings were passed throughout the South in the 1830's. The Vigilance Association in South Carolina's capital, Columbia, published a $1500 reward in the newspaper for the capture of those who handed out abolitionist writings, especially copies of William Lloyd Garrison's *The Liberator* and Walker's pamphlet. Georgia's 1835 law imposed the death penalty for abolitionist writings, called "incendiary documents."

Though almost all slaves were, as the law and custom required, kept illiterate, it was known that a slave who could read would pass around knowledge of the agitation against slavery in the North, perhaps derived from the angry and alarmist Southern newspapers, or inflammatory handbills, or speeches of opponents of slavery in Congress, or abolition books, pamphlets, monthlies or even handkerchiefs. An observer noted in 1836, "[a] sufficient number of these can read to enable them to obtain all the information from the newspapers which they perceive to be interesting to them, and through ten thousand channels of oral communication, such information is extended until it reaches the most ignorant slave, upon the most remote and secluded plantation." This fear held by the slaveholders was no doubt exaggerated, and ignored the independent will to resist of the slaves and the mounting greed and hunger for power and territory of the slaveholders. For the peak of the slave patrols (1830-1861), and the peak of the repressive laws against blacks (1830-1850), came as the regime of the large slaveholders, led by the raw cotton barons, took hold. U.S. cotton production was half a million bales in 1822; by 1860, it was five million. The ascendancy of "a closed oligarchy with a political policy" struggling to control national policy was hardened and complete by 1850, and this is the main explanation for the state laws and local attitudes that clamped down on the transmission of the alphabet on every farm.

Yet, a large increase in anti-slavery societies in the North and a ramping-up of production of abolitionist writings did take place by 1840. A report in 1837 of the American Anti-Slavery Society described the publication of four monthlies totaling 75,000 copies per month in 1836 - a nine-fold increase over the prior year. And anti-slavery writings did get around among literate slaves. A fugitive slave remembered: "After I had learned to read, I was very fond of reading newspapers, when I could get them. One day in the year 1830, I picked up a piece of old newspaper containing the speech of J.Q. Adams, in the U.S. Senate, upon a petition of the ladies of Massachusetts, praying for the abolition of slavery in the District of Columbia. This I kept hid away for some months, and read it until it was so worn I could scarce make out the letters." The risk to slaveowners, they felt, derived from Northern books, like *Uncle Tom's Cabin*. A book like that, an 1854 slave manual said, "does injury to the slave, by making it the duty of owners, to prevent the circulation of the book among them, and requiring a more rigid police for that purpose."

B. Slave Religion

Much of slave religion was of the hidden kind and in the countryside; there, it was a mixture of African beliefs and traditions with those of the Christians, resulting in a new creation in the songs and lamentations within the cabins of the slave quarters, in the nearby woods, the cane thickets, in the ravines along the banks of streams, rivers, ponds and creeks, and by the reeds of the swamps. Loud drumming, singing and dancing were the African style of worship; the laws and patrols sought to silence it.

Thus, much of slave religion and the daily and nightly solemnity of slave prayers about the tribulations of the slaves was forced to be invisible, or tried to be; it had to fear the patrols. Wash Wilson, once a slave, recalled: "When de [slaves] go round singin' 'Steal Away to Jesus,' dat mean dere gwine be a 'ligious meetin' dat night. De masters . . . didn't like dem 'ligious meetin's so us natcherly slips off at night, down in de bottoms or somewhere. Sometimes us sing and pray all night."

The religion of the slaveholders, if they had one, always boiled down to one theme: obey your masters. So, in secret: "My father would have church in dwelling houses and they had to whisper. [. . .] Sometimes they would have church at his house. That would be when they would want a real meetin' with some real preachin'. [. . .] They used to sing their songs in a whisper and pray in a whisper. That was a prayer-meeting from house to house once or twice - once or twice a week."

Where slave religion was tolerated or supported, the black preacher, whether free or slave, was central. The great scholar of slave life and U.S. history, W.E.B. DuBois, wrote that "[t]hree things characterized this religion of the slave, - the Preacher, the Music, and the Frenzy." The black preacher, DuBois said, was "bard, physician, judge, and priest." The black preacher, too, Dubois said, was a "leader, a politician, an orator, a 'boss,' an intriguer, [and] an idealist."

Many slaveholders supported the idea of Christianizing the slaves. "The day 'fore one of dem big baptizings dey 'dammed up de crick a little, and when dey gathered 'round de pool next day there was some tall shoutin' and singin'," Mahala Jewel, a former slave recalled.

Prayer meetings might be allowed by slaveholders. Walter Calloway, a former slave in Alabama, recalled: "Same time Marse John buy mammy an' us boys, he buy a black man name Joe. He a preacher an' de marster let de slaves build a brush arbor in de pecan grove over in de big pastur', an' when de weather warn't too cold all de slaves was 'lowed to meet there on Sunday for preachin'."

Aunt Easter Jackson, a former slave in Georgia, remembered her devotion:

> Then there were the prayer meetin's, once a week, first on one of the

plantations den another; when all de [slaves] would meet and worship, singin' praises unto the Lord; I can hear 'em now, dere voices soundin' far away. Yes sir! Folks had religion in dem days, the Old Time Religion. Our white folks belonged to the First Baptist Church in Laarange, and all de slaves went to de same church. Our services wus in de basement.

Many plantations allowed, encouraged or even mandated slave religion, as long as it was of a pre-approved Christian flavor. In the slave quarters, Harry Smith, a former slave, wrote: "After eating, often preaching and prayer meetings by some of the old folks in some of the cabins and in other fiddles would ring out. It was a scene never to be forgotten, as the old christians sing and pray until four in the morning, while at the other cabins many would be patting, singing and dancing."

A former slave in Texas, Mose Hursey, recalled:

On Sundays they a meetin', sometimes at our house, sometimes at 'nother house. [. . .] They'd preach and pray and sing - shout, too. I heard them git up with a powerful force of the spirit, clappin' they hands and walkin' around the place. They'd shout, "I got the glory. I got that old time 'ligion I my heart." I see some powerful 'figurations of the spirit in them days.

The new black Protestants of the South worshiped with "[p]rayer meetings, shouting, and spirituals." The slave quarters, too, were home to "conjure, herbalism, ghost lore, witchcraft, and fortune-telling." Conjurers - called, at the time, "hoodoo" and "witch men" - were respected and feared for their power to set a "fix" on someone; their crooked canes, charms, roots, toads' heads, scorpions, spider blood, graveyard dirt, love powders, herbal cures and other 'bad medicines' were the tools of the trade. Conjurers were often asked to help the slave this way: to escape the patrols.

C.   Why Go off the Plantation without a Pass?

If a slave could get a pass, he or she could visit friends and relatives, mainly on Saturday nights and Sundays. Here's a description from Jefferson Franklin

Henry, a former slave in Georgia. "Oh! How they did frolic 'round Sadday night when they could git passes. Sundays they went to church but not without a pass for, if they ever was cotch out without one, them paterollers would beat 'em up something terrible."

There was music on Saturday nights: "On Saturday nights we'd sing and dance and we made our own instruments, which was gourd fiddles and quill flutes." And homemade banjos, too. "The banjo is an African instrument, made from the half of a fruit called the calabash, or gourd, which has a very hard rind. A thin skin or piece of bladder is stretched over the opening, and over this one or two strings are stretched, which are raised on a bridge. The banjo is the negroes' guitar, and certainly it is the first-born among stringed instruments."

Many now-forgotten reasons for slaves to leave the plantation fall under a mundane category of day to day life: running errands. "I've hid many a night in the fence corners where I'd be agoin' somewhere to get my mammy tobacco." A slave memory of less mundane reasons:

> The slaves would have their parties and
> dances. Slaves would gather from

various plantations and these parties would sometimes last all night. It was customary for the slaves to get passes from their masters permitting them to attend, but sometimes passes were not given for reasons. In line with these parties it is remembered that there existed at that time what was known as the Paddle-Rollers, these so-called Paddle-Rollers was made up of a bunch of white boys who would sneak up on these defenseless negroes unawares late in the night and demand that all show their passes. Those that could not show passes were whipped, both the negro girls and boys alike.

Why did enslaved men go to another plantation without a pass? The main reason was simply to visit friends, relatives, wives, children and girlfriends. Wives and girlfriends were likely to live on other plantations - wives and husbands often did not live under the same roof. "Courtin' some gal" was the "mostest reason" for a male slave to be out at night. As one male former slave from Texas said, "but I'd go to see dat gal every time, patter rolls or no patter rolls."

A recollection: "Courtin' folks got caught and beat up by the patter-rollers more than anybody else, because they were always slipping out to meet one another at night." A woman's memory: "Patroller, you ask me? I do remember them. Wasn't I a goodlookin' woman? Didn't Sam want to see me more than twice a week? Wouldn't he risk it without the pass some time? Sure he did. The patrollers got after and run Sam many a time."

Marriage, however, was no defense. "I have known the husband thus chastised for being found in company with his wife, if he was not able to produce his pass or permit to visit her that night."

One of the purposes of whipping a slave in front of a girlfriend or wife is often forgotten - humiliation in front of other slaves. A fugitive slave risked the patrols while courting a woman. He was brought on a false charge before a judge. To his surprise, he saw "the girl I was courting, brought there for the purpose of humbling my pride, and mortifying me. For you must think, reader, that it would be rather mortifying to be stripped and flogged in the presence of a girl."

An 1854 essay on "The Treatment and Management of Slaves" discussed the problem of slaves loving slaves on other plantations. Marriage between such slaves should not be prohibited, yet it should be avoided: "they cannot live together as they ought, and are constantly liable to separation, in the changing of property." Yes; the "changing of property" destroyed relationships and families daily, even on a whim. One account will do. A major slaveholder was losing in billiards, staked six slaves on a bet to a New Orleans gambler, and lost. The slaves, two boys and four girls, were put on a train - kids separated for life from parents, grandparents, brothers and sisters.

As a result of the regular "changing of property," the white physicians of the time diagnosed a disease peculiar to the slaves: "Longing for home generates a distinct malady, known to physicians as Nostalgia." Relationships between slaves on different plantations were so common, that many, perhaps most, slaveowners preferred it: "the masters think it unwise to have slave families live together, where they can witness the punishments inflicted on each other. It has a tendency to make them discontented."

D.   Examples of Passes

Passes were handwritten, and required literacy by writer and reader. Passes could not be read, or written, by an illiterate slave. Passes could not be read by illiterate patrollers: accounts show that the patrol captain was often called upon to read a pass.

Any white man was allowed, in practice, to write a pass. In one instance, a male slave on the run had a fake pass, but lost it in the swamps. A new one was signed by a few white cattle drivers that the slave met along the way:

> John Roper, a very interesting young lad, whom I have seen and traveled with for eighty or ninety miles on his road from Florida, is a free man, descended from Indian and white. I trust, he will be allowed to pass on without interruption, being convinced from what I have seen that he is free, and though dark, is not an African. I had seen his papers before they were wetted.

John Brown, while a slave, got a pass "from a poor white man, for which I gave him an old hen."

The children of slaveowners often wrote passes. A former general in Missouri recalled: "It is melancholy to remember, as the thought now obtrudes itself, that Uncle Toby, Uncle Jack, and other gray-haired men and women, as well as the younger ones, were compelled to have written permission to leave home, and would come even to me, a little child, when the older members of the family were too busy, to give them a written pass to go to town."

The passes were handwritten notes. Here is one: "My Boy Mack has my Permission to sleep in a house in Bedon's Alley, hired by his Mother. This ticket is good for two months from this date Sarah H. Savage September 19th, 1843."

South Carolina's law back in 1740 helpfully provided a sample form: "Permit this slave to be absent from the plantation of A.B. until _____."

There were obvious difficulties if the slaveowner was illiterate - a common occurrence. One method of handling this problem was to give the patrols a list of slaves from each plantation and task the patrols with taking attendance of the slaves. If slaves were missing, the patrols called upon the slaveowner to see if the slave was gone by "special permit or knowledge"; if not, the slave was guilty of the crime of leaving the plantation without a pass. One account said: "The older negroes still tell how they were accustomed to line up for the roll call when the patroller came to the plantation."

The passes had the power to name. The pass had to have the name of the slave on it - but what if the slave was in the middle of escaping? John Brown, who later learned to write and published his account of life as a slave in Georgia and Alabama, got his name from a pass written by a friendly person during his escape. "I got a rest at his dwelling, and induced him to get me a free pass, for which I made him take an old watch. With that pass I assumed the name of John Brown, which I have retained ever since."

E.   What Happened if a Slave Was Caught without a Pass?

If caught without a pass, the slave faced beatings and whippings, on the spot. In Lynchburg, Virginia, the patrols used a "fenced in whippin' post" if a slave was caught without a pass. One former slave recalled getting caught by the patrol: "they stretches me over a log and hits thirty-nine licks with a rawhide loaded with rock, and every time they hit me the blood and hide done fly." Harriet Jacobs recalled what she saw: "Everywhere men, women and children were whipped till the blood stood in puddles at their feet. Some received five hundred lashes; others were tied, hands and feet, and tortured with a bucking paddle, which blisters the feet terribly." One patroller said that he "sometimes caught and flogged four in a night." Sizeable gatherings resulted in sizeable whippings. A dance outside Louisville was described this way: "The patrollers came there that night, about twelve of them, there being about one hundred and fifty colored people at the dance. They whipped about fifty that night who were so unfortunate as not to have a pass."

Laws limited, with macabre logic, the amount of lashes, often to fifteen, or twenty, or thirty-nine; but the patrols did not "stop for the law, and if they tie a man up, he is very well off if he gets only two hundred." The whippings were "without judge or jury, and with no other limit to the severity of the infliction, than such as the drunken caprice of the patrols may prescribe." The cold, statutory, silent mathematics of whipping by patrols in the written laws conceals the angry, red, loud reality. A former slave recalled in

1853: "The law says you may give a slave thirty-nine lashes if he is found roaming about without a pass. I warrant that ten with the bull-whip, properly laid on, will cut any man's life out; and this is twenty-nine 'licks' within the law." Often, a slave caught without a pass was hauled off and confined, or taken to the guard house, or jail; he would later be picked up by or delivered to his owner, in return for capture and incarceration fees. If a runaway slave happened to be caught at the end of the day, that slave might be sold before he was claimed by an owner - a lucrative day for the patroller, who "considers it a god-send to meet an unknown negro without a pass." Mississippi provided that a slave picked up without a pass more than eight miles away from home was to be treated as a runaway and the catcher paid $30, to be paid, in part, by the slaveowner.

Since the patrollers were on horseback, and unlikely to offer to share the saddle with a slave, the slaves were roped to the saddle and had to run alongside or behind the horse. "I saw horsemen with some poor panting negro tied to their saddles, and compelled by the lash to keep up with their speed, till they arrived at the jail yard." Or in front. A memory of a slave returned to an owner by the patrol: "There was six white men and ten hounds. All the white men was on horses, and poor Hattie was in front barefooted, the dogs behind her. Hattie was almost naked that morning; blood was all on her feet as she was walking along. I saw all of it with my own two eyes."

Here, questions about the dogs might be raised. "No particular breed of dogs is needed for hunting negroes: blood-hounds, fox-hounds, bull-dogs, and curs were used." Training skills began early, as "they are shut up when puppies, and never allowed to see a negro, except while training to catch him."

The patrols were feared and despised by blacks throughout the South - one memory of a former slave will do.

> Who are the patrols? They are men appointed by the county courts to look after slaves without a pass. They have almost unlimited power over the slaves. They are the sons of run-down families. The greatest scoundrel is always captain of the band of patrols. They are the off-scouring of all things, the refuse . . . the ears and tails of slavery, the scales

and fins of fish. Like starved wharf rats, they are out nights, creeping into slave cabins, to see if they have an old bone there; drive out husbands from their own beds, and then take their places. They get up all sort of pretenses, false as their lying tongues can make them, and then whip the slaves and carry a gory lash to the master, for a piece of bread.

Aside from the powers to stop, search, whip and arrest that were placed in writing in state and municipal laws, the excesses of the patrols were also feared by the slaves: drunken, angry abandon. Slave women were vulnerable: "Many women hid themselves in woods and swamps, to keep out of their way. If any of the husbands or fathers told of these outrages, they were tied up to the public whipping post, and cruelly scourged for telling lies about white men." The "females fear every indignity the ruffians may please to perpetrate." The patrols, at all times, had the legal advantage that a slave could not testify against a white person, and the practical advantage that the slaves had no one to complain to - except their own owner. And the patrols also had the cultural advantage that the bodies of black women were the schools of white male sexuality throughout the slave states.

The laws made it impossible to resist the patrollers, even verbally. Rowan County, North Carolina, gave each patroller the "power to seize any negro slave who behaves insolently to a patroller." This was not unusual; Tennessee's law, a typical one, against riots and unlawful assemblies, also included this crime: "any insulting or provoking language used by a slave to any white person."

Also, the patrols were known to plant evidence. "In some cases the searchers scattered powder and shot among their clothes, and then sent other parties to find them, and bring them forward as proof that they were plotting insurrection." In addition, the patrols robbed the slaves: "The dwellings of the colored people, unless they happened to be protected by some influential white person, who was nigh [near] at hand, were robbed of clothing and everything else the marauders thought worth carrying away."

F.   Necessity of Illiteracy and Slave Defiance

A literate slave could leave the plantation, read the limited road posts and signs of the time, and escape. Lewis Clarke recounted that he and another slave plotted to steal a horse and a pony and escape; on the road, Lewis Clarke planned to pose as a master and the other man as slave. After going five miles, Lewis Clarke gave up the plan because he thought that he would have been noticed as a fake master because he could not read the "guideboards": "ignorant as people are in Kentucky, they would have thought it strange to see a man with a [servant], who could not read a guideboard." 'Guideboards,' or guideposts, or 'finger-boards,' stretched between county seats. They required a small amount of reading and counting - counting miles engraved in wood that told the distance from one place to another - skills denied the slaves.

Frederick Douglass in 1850 described education as "perhaps the most dangerous" of the "menacing influences." He was a man who learned to read from young white playmates. When, in 1834, South Carolina tightened its prohibition against the teaching of reading and writing to slaves, one argument in opposition was simple: it is the white children who teach this. "Again, who is it that teach your slaves to read? It is generally done by the children of the owners. Who would tolerate an indictment against his son or daughter for teaching a favorite slave to read?" Whether by slate, pencil, pens made of pine tree bark, or chalk, and normally by stealth, the rudiments of literacy were cobbled together by pre-Civil War slaves. And in their absence: "I had no slate, so I used to write on the ground."

Slaves could turn to secretly literate slaves, but the process was too informal to have sticking power. A former slave in North Carolina recalled that he, as a child, knew of another boy who was a slave "who was terrible smart. He learn to read an' write. He take other colored children out in the fields and teach 'em about the Bible, but they forgit it 'fore the next Sunday."

The worst document that a slave could write proved that he was a free man. This was hard to do, as emancipation required government (court) approval, and thus the documents were much more complicated than a simple pass, but "free papers" were forged anyway, despite the heavy fines: a minimum of 5 years in prison in Alabama, with a maximum of 25 years. One secretly-literate man, married, with children, to a woman on another plantation, decided to run away after his owner had vetoed all marriages with slaves on other plantations and arranged marriages for his slaves by fiat. Nearby lived a free black man. "I got him to let me see his free papers and copied every word of them." He hid them in his cabin, with two pictures, letters, and "some old passes, books, and [news]papers." The overseer discovered them in a search for a runaway, and the secretly-literate slave was sold in two days.

Another reason for mandatory illiteracy among slaves was a problem peculiar to the cities, where slaveowners punished a slave by whipping but, over time, delegated the task to city jailers. The system relied on written documents, as in this account of New Orleans. "Nothing is more common here, than for the masters and mistresses of slaves, when they wish them, either male or female, to be punished, to send them to the prison, with a note to the gaoler, specifying the number of lashes to be inflicted. The slave must carry back a note to his master, telling him that the punishment has been inflicted." It was a system waiting to fail if the slave was literate, for the literate slave could write a jailer-note for himself.

Reading was a skill learned in secret and kept secret. Thomas Jones, while a young slave, got ahold of a spelling book and "hid my book with the utmost care under some liquor barrels in the smoke house." He worked in a store, and was almost caught reading in the back by his owner, so he tossed his spelling book behind the barrels. The owner whipped him to find out what he had thrown, accusing him of theft; "I knew if my book was discovered all was lost, and I felt prepared for any hazard or suffering rather than give up my book and my hopes of improvement." Thomas Jones did not tell about the spelling book and retrieved it after the whipping. This occurred soon after he had learned to write his name in block letters.

Belle Myers Carothers was kicked by her owner when he saw her learning the alphabet while watching the owner's baby play with alphabet blocks. This did not stop her, and she also used a speller she had found. Later, she recalled, "I found a hymn book, and spelled out 'When I Can Read My Title Clear.' I was so happy when I saw that I could really read, that I ran around telling all the other slaves."

John Thompson was a fugitive slave when he wrote his autobiography. As a boy, he was sent in the morning along with the white children to the schoolhouse, carrying their lunches. One of the children, Henry, taught John Thompson how to read in the woods, outside the sight of the other children and passerby. "I soon got through my first book, after which Henry bought me the Introduction to the English Reader."

A slave who lived in Augusta told of living on a plantation as a child near a schoolhouse for white children. "The well is close by, and when I used to go for water I got the boys to teach me a letter at a time. I used to give them nuts and things to teach me."

One more example of secretly engaging in the defiant act of learning to read: this example is of Henry O'Neal Turner, born a free man in South Carolina, who later became the first black chaplain in the Union Army, and a national church leader. At the age of twelve, "only three colored men of his acquaintance could read a little in the Bible and hymn book." Then, he "procured a spelling book, and an old white lady and a white boy with whom he played, taught him the alphabet and how to spell as far as two syllables," but the white boy's father put a stop to the lessons. Turner's next tutor was an old black man "who did not know a letter but was a prodigy in sounds," who helped him get half-way through "old Webster's spelling book." Finally, at fifteen, Turner got a job with lawyers, who were so impressed by his memory, that they taught him history, law, math - even astronomy.

Reading was bad; writing was worse: again, secrecy was the norm. An emancipated slave recalled: "I could do my own writing, unbeknown to the overseer, and carry my own pass." The simplest forged pass was for a visit to a nearby plantation. A former slave recalled: "As I could read and write I used to write out passes for myself, so I could go and see my old wife; and I wrote passes for the other men on the place, so they could go and see their wives that lived off the place." An advertisement for a runaway twenty-year old female slave in 1845 said that she "is rather tall; can read or write, and so forge passes for herself." Another advertisement said: "can write a pretty hand and has probably forged a pass." A forged pass might also allow an escape: a former slave recounted forging three passes and using them successfully on his escape from Memphis to Cincinnati and on to Canada.

VII. The Effects of the Laws

Slaves might help each other to run away; slaves might organize to rebel; slaves might forge passes: these fears led to laws about drums, dancing, reading, writing, partying, and praying.

By 1740, South Carolina levied fines against slaveowners who allowed slaves to beat drums or blow horns. More laws concerning communication between slaves were later codified. Georgia's 1770 law said that "all due care [must] be taken to restrain the wandering and meeting of negroes and other slaves at all times, and more especially on Saturday nights, Sundays, and other holy-days, and their using and carrying . . . weapons, or using and keeping drums, horns, and other loud instruments, which may call together or give sign or notice to one another of their wicked designs and intentions." Drums had been banned - due to fear of rebel communication - in other English colonies, such as Barbados, as early as 1676.

The laws specified the dangerous times of the week and the year: Saturday nights, Sundays, and Christmas week.

New Orleans banned religious worship by blacks at night in 1832. Today, church services are mainly a day-time thing; then, services - on any day but Sunday - for all in America began at sunset, because work stopped at sunset. As a British observer noted in 1833: "meetings of the people for political or religious purposes are generally called in the United States during the two or three summer months, not at any particular hour, but at sun-down." Thus, restrictions after sundown fell hard on those who worked the latest - free blacks and slaves.

Free blacks were tightly regulated - though full free citizens, there was no talk of Constitutional rights, or other fantasies. Virginia, in 1805, prohibited state guardians of free black orphans from requiring that adopters of the children "teach such orphan reading, writing or arithmetic." The laws governing the movement, education and even presence of free blacks battened down in the 1820-1850 period. The ambitious nature of the crackdown on free blacks is even more remarkable given the fact that, by 1850, perhaps one-half of free blacks in the South were literate.

Cities passed detailed laws on the conduct of slaves and free blacks that were mainly aimed at the limited freedoms of Saturday nights, Sundays and holidays. Charleston banned dancing by slaves in 1813. Disturbing the peace, in Charleston, included "singing, whooping, or other obstreperous, wanton and unnecessary noises, either in the daytime or at night." An 1834 editorial from the Charleston Courier complained that the patrol was becoming ineffective just beyond the city limits. The editorial listed the evils that needed better patrols: "drunken and riotous negroes pitching cents, and playing marbles, cursing and blaspheming in the vicinity of the ruinous and fatal sons of vice, the retail liquor shops." Charleston criminalized the playing of cards and dice games in public; the stakes belonged to any white person "seizing the same." In 1835, St. Louis made it unlawful, after 9:00 p.m., for slaves or free blacks to attend "any ball, dance or religious assemblage."

The laws against the literacy of slaves were not just meant to prevent escapes, but to suppress even the desire for freedom. If a slave wanted to write, say to a relative on another plantation, "[t]he white people had to write and read all the letters that passed between us." The dominant everyday message, from Congress to the statehouse, from the churches to the farms, was that there was no other way of life than slavery, and illiteracy ensured that nothing challenged that message.

Many slaves were lucky enough to live on a plantation where the slaveowner, or more likely his wife or kids, wanted to teach him or her to read. Memoirs by women slaveholders after the Civil War, and interviews with former slaves, suggest that the religious teachings of the women slaveholders, and the less common task of teaching their slaves to read, were mainly efforts in the Upper South - Maryland, Virginia, Missouri, and Kentucky. The Deep South, with its large cotton plantations, the large coastal South Carolina and Georgia rice plantations, and the riverside, cane-brake sugar plantations of Louisiana, all with large, isolated workforces, were less likely areas for Missus to preach or teach.

Secret learning, and secret writing, was the order of the day. "For God's sake don't let a slave be cotched with pencil or paper," one former slave recalled, "that was a major crime; you might as well have killed your master or mistress." All along, in many states, teaching slaves had been banned, as in Georgia, where no one "was lawfully permitted to give book instruction to slaves, even in any one of the three R's." Even free blacks in the cities could no longer go to school, or be taught to read or write, again as in Georgia, where, after 1830, "all Negro schools were clandestine." The laws were effective: a former slave considered how many slaves she had met who could read and write: "I never saw more than three or four that could properly read at all. I never saw but one that could write." The author of an extensive survey of religion among blacks in the U.S., the pro-slavery pastor Charles Colcock Jones, wrote in 1842:

> It is impossible to form an estimate of the number of Negroes that read. My belief is that the proportion would be expressed by an almost inconceivable fraction. The greatest number of readers is found in and about towns and cities, and among the free Negro population, some two or three generations removed from servitude.

An abolitionist from Ohio, after a tour of the South, wrote:

> On the plantation where I now reside there are about one hundred persons over the age of twelve, not a soul of whom can read or write. The same is the case with a large proportion of the plantations throughout the country. I am perfectly safe in saying that, including house-servants and all, both in town and country, there is not one in fifty of the slave population of the South that can read or write.

All estimates of slave literacy at the time are low: an observer in Georgia estimated that 5,000 of 400,000 slaves could read and write. Considering the swift and certain punishments meted out for infractions of the law - and the threat of immediate sale - it is no wonder that slaves learned to fear newspapers. A woman who was once a slave recalled that the slaves were "more scared of newspapers than they is of snakes now, and us never known what a Bible was in them days."

Attitudes of fellow slaves could be a barrier to learning to read the Bible. One man, taught to read by the wife of a nearby plantation owner, recalled that learning to read exposed him to "ridicule on the part of my fellow-slaves, who thought it very foolish of me to attempt to learn to read 'the white men's book.'"

Reading and writing were signs of intelligence, and intelligence might lead to thoughts of Philadelphia or Michigan or Ohio or Quakers or even Canada and freedom. Thus, intelligence in a slave became a bad trait - a reflection, again, of the centrality of the new domination of the slave gang workforce: once prized traits on small farms and in towns and cities had become unnecessary and a potential security threat.

But the most rigorous examinations of slaves by those slave inspectors, is on the mental capacity. If they are found to be very intelligent, this is pronounced the most objectionable of all other qualities in the life of a slave. In fact, it undermines the whole fabric of his chattelhood; it prepares for what slaveholders are pleased to pronounce the unpardonable sin when committed by a slave. It lays the foundation for running away and going to Canada. They also see in it a love for freedom, patriotism, insurrection, bloodshed and exterminating war against American slavery.

This was true in the countryside, where the vast bulk of slaves lived; in the cities, literacy was still however, often valued by slaveholders - for example, the price of a slave in New Orleans, hired out as a waiter to a hotel, was higher for slaves who could read and write. It could be said of Augusta, "[i]t is not unusual to see slaves reading newspapers, and familiar with the current news of the day."

Intelligence and literacy had been valued in slaves in the second half of the 18th century throughout the slave states; as slavery expanded in the new century, however, attitudes and laws grew so hostile to the education of slaves, and even to free blacks, that education became a police matter. In 1799, a slave in North Carolina was given his freedom and a pension by the legislature for discovering a cure for the bite of a rattlesnake. In 1803, Thomas

Jefferson invited the son of free black farmers, who had become an astronomer and written the first almanac in America, to Monticello. Both of these examples were inconceivable just two decades later.

The step from reading to writing was a major one. Noah Davis was born a slave in Virginia, became a preacher, earned his freedom, and then became a preacher in Baltimore. His father had learned to read and taught him the alphabet from a spelling book. As a young man, he worked for a shoemaker. "The first idea I ever got of writing, was from trying to imitate my employer, who used to write the names of his customers on the lining of the boots and shoes, as he gave them out to be made. So I tried to make letters, and soon succeeded in writing my name, and then the word Fredericksburg, and so on." The local preachers had a habit of reading a chapter from the Bible before services started. "If he named the chapter before reading it, I would soon find it. In this way, I gathered much information in pronouncing many hard words in the Scriptures."

The reaction against rebellion and abolition, and the necessity of securing larger slave workforces, as much as it involved high politics - federal questions

- also reached down to the hour by hour lives of the slaves - 'an invasion of the whole man' - and thereby broadened the reach of the patrols.

White attitudes favored illiteracy among slaves. Thus, it could be written in Georgia in 1842 that "the statutes of our respective Slave states forbid all knowledge of letters to the Negroes; and where the statutes do not, custom does."

The dramatic increase in repression after 1830 had its desired effect, thereafter. "On plantations of hundreds of slaves it was common to discover that not one of them had the mere rudiments of education. In some large districts it was considered almost a phenomenon to find a Negro who could read the Bible or sign his name." In Georgia, a study concluded that "outside of Savannah, Augusta and Columbus there were, it is said, not a dozen colored people able to read and write, and in the country places, perhaps not one."

North Carolina's experience was typical. The state legislature rejected bills to prohibit the teaching of slaves to read or write in 1818, 1819, and 1825. In 1826, the Governor told the legislature that the Northern agitation "demanded from us a sleepless vigilance" and he recommended laws expanding the powers of the patrols, which was finally done in the legislature of 1828-1829. The ban on teaching a slave to read or write was considered by North Carolina's Senate in secret session; the ban began in 1830, the beginning of the height of the slave power.

"But this mighty power, through the press and the schools, and the rival political parties, and penal legislation, and the terrors of persecution, at last issued its mandates; bade men hold their tongues, and utter no blasphemy against the immaculate purity of that august power."

The slave power could silence the voices of criticism, not just from blacks and abolitionists, but from the churches, and the churches grew silent. After the Civil War, a Methodist preacher in Georgia wrote, "You know that the slave power, that held even Congress subject to its will, and could lay its restraining hand upon the Supreme Court of the United States, and, in defiance of legislative enactments of Northern States, send an officer and bring back the fugitive slave, would have silenced their voices forever had they presumed to preach against all the abuses of slavery." He concluded, "Our minds, our speech, our consciences, our press, our pulpit, all were in abject dependence upon the slave power."

The fact that fear of the abolitionist movement led to increased powers of the patrols was well known. A pro-slavery book in 1836 argued, "The inquisitorial visits, patrols, searches, confinement to plantations, the refusal of usual indulgences, and the exaction of additional duties, are all the fruits of [abolitionist] fanaticism."

It is frightful just how successful the blunt laws banning the education of slaves were, especially after the Nat Turner rebellion: the measure of the success was the almost total collapse of instruction in reading or writing; all formal religious instruction became oral. "The word instruction thereafter signified among the southerners a procedure quite different from what the term meant in the seventeenth and eighteenth centuries, when negroes were taught to read and write that they might learn the truth for themselves." This now meant "a scheme of oral instruction in Christian truth or of religion without letters." The missionaries' work on the plantations, and their Sunday schools for children and adult slaves, had always been mainly oral instruction, but all efforts at literacy were constrained by 1831. "Memory training," without letters, now ruled the day, outside the always modestly-sized Catholic or Quaker settlements.

No longer were the souls of the slaves - thought to require literacy so that the Bible might be read - all that important; the new goal was moderation over long periods of time by the slaveowners, while the slaves were kept far from the alphabet. "The goal of Christianity was to make slaveholders more godly."

The raw quantity of literacy among slaveowners themselves is often overstated. Slaveowners on the large plantations - the Southern aristocratic core of the slave power - were more likely literate, and more likely to have literate house-slaves - but even there, books were few. An annual get-together of slaveowners in New Orleans was described this way: "From all the neighboring states the planters come in with their wives and daughters, and spend one or more weeks, or even months, in dancing, fiddling, flirting, smoking cigars, and abusing abolitionists." For the great bulk of slaveholders - those with ten slaves or less - literacy was rare, and not nearly as valued as saddles and rifles. An author who toured the slave states noted that "the slaveholders in the planting districts are quite as destitute of learning as the poor whites," citing a survey of one county where, of 21 slave-owning families, only one married couple could read. The Governor of Virginia said in 1839 that a quarter of whites could not write their names on marriage certificates.

The census figures of the time peg the numbers of literate whites over the age of 20 in the slave states as between 70 and 90%; in 1860, by contrast, the census simply listed 0% of the 1.7 million adult slaves as literate.

Forced mass illiteracy - of millions of slave men and women, and their children - worked. A former Georgian slave, John Brown, who later wrote a book about his life, did not, as a slave, know where he was: "my mind was bent upon making tracks for England, which I fancied was not very far away," though he was close to the Blue Ridge mountains. During one escape, he "made for the high road, which I thought would lead me straight to England." A white man in Tennessee asked for his pass, said that it was a forgery because it did not have multiple signatures, and tricked him, before returning him to his owner. John Brown later escaped to Canada and one day did make it to England.

The forced imposition of illiteracy extended to religious teaching, and the patrols were watching. The son of a Virginian slaveowner recalled: "Two or three ladies whom I knew met on Sunday afternoon to teach some Negro children; they had not so met three times before they were dispersed by the authorities, although it appeared that they had only given the children oral and religious instruction." Another memory: "We would hold weekly prayer meetings at the different farms we worked at. Many times the patrols would catch us as we were going, and after whipping us we would be sent back." The patrols broke up prayer meetings and scourged those who attended even where not required by law: "While the laws in certain places were not so drastic as to prohibit religious assemblies, the same was effected by patrols and mobs."

The security issues faced by slaveowners were these: prayer meetings could be boisterous and thus unnerving; prayer meetings were meetings; prayer meetings were an attempt to create an independent sacred space; and prayer meetings might - perhaps always would, and always did - lead, with hands up, open wide, to prayers for freedom. On this last point, the fear of the owners may have been grounded in stubborn and universal fact. "We used to slip off in the woods in the old slave days on Sunday evening way down in the swamps to sing and pray to our own liking. We prayed for this day of freedom. We come from four and five miles to pray together that if we don't live to see it, to please let our chillen live to see a better day and be free."

The fevered push against religious gatherings of free blacks and slaves resulted in mass arrests. In Charleston alone, 469 free blacks and slaves were arrested at one church meeting in 1817, followed by an arrest of 144 on a Sunday afternoon the following year.

Menacing laws throughout the slave states required either the presence of whites at religious gatherings of slaves, a majority of whites, or the presence of an "official"- likely, outside the cities, a patroller. Two slaves were convicted in Missouri in 1854 for "preaching to their fellows, with no officer present." The laws and the patrols did not stop slaves from organizing underground religious meetings for their lamentations. "We would sneak off and have prayer meetin'. Sometimes the paddyrollers catch us and beat us good but that didn't keep us from tryin.'" Attendance at the modest above-ground churches was difficult for slaves and often ill-attended. "There are multitudes of districts in the South and Southwest, in which the churches cannot contain one-tenth of the Negro population; besides others in which there are no churches at all. It must be remembered also that in many of those churches there is preaching only once a fortnight, or once a month, and then perhaps only one sermon."

The abolition movement was also blamed for the decline in evangelization and religious instruction of blacks by missionaries throughout the South in the final decades before the Civil War. "It was considered best to disband schools and discontinue meetings, at least for a season," concluded a missionary. By 1835, a white revival in the South was over; the churches retreated from teaching all blacks. A meeting of white citizens in Charleston formally thanked the clergy of that city for promptly "responding to public sentiment" by "suspending their schools in which the free colored population were taught." It could be said by missionaries in 1840 that "abolition excitement, then at white heat" had led to "the cold shoulder."

Religious actions - praying, singing hymns, meeting, teaching, reading - were the bane of the patrols, not to mention the 'incendiary' substance of much of Christian and African religious teaching.

"You said something about how we served God. Marster's slaves met and worshiped from house to house, and honey, we talked to God all us wanted. You would get a remit [pass] to go to these places. You would have to show your remit. If the pattyrollers caught you, they would whip you." The patrols "go through their respective towns to prevent slaves from meeting for religious worship or religious instruction." One patroller recalled that there was a fear, just before Christmas in South Carolina in 1830, that the slaves were going to rise on Christmas day. Patrols went out, and "orders were given to search every negro house for books or prints of any kind, and Bibles and Hymn books were particularly mentioned. And should we find any, our orders were to inflict punishment by whipping the slave until he informed who gave them to him, or how he came by them." This hostility to religion, whether African, Islamic, or

Christian, was not, of course, always successful, despite the bans on literacy: "It was always a mystery to the white brethren how the slaves could line out hymns, preach Christ and redemption, yet have no knowledge even of how the name of Christ was spelled."

Slaves often went to the church of their owner in, naturally, a dutifully segregated manner, with blacks in the gallery, or basement, or their own section, known as the "negro pew." "In the ceremony of the Lord's supper, after the whites had partaken, the sacrament was administered to the negro members." Many slaveowners taught Christianity, in one way or another, to their slaves. But, as a physician who authored a treatise on slave management wrote, those efforts were weak and commenced "perhaps with a zeal too languid for the end proposed, being accompanied by the ridicule of others of the society."

Regular churchgoing by slaveowners, like their level of literacy, should not be overstated, especially outside the largest cities. A tract about churchgoing by whites in North Carolina said, in 1854: "Three-fourths of the people are destitute of public services on the Sabbath; and that about one-third of the parents can read and write, cast accounts, and gauge a barrel of brandy." Inside Georgia, it was remarked: "There was not a settled minister of the gospel, of any denomination, who preached constantly at the same place, for more than two hundred miles, on the stage road leading from the coast to the capital; and yet, in each of those counties, from six to thirteen churches are returned in the census." A pro-slavery dissertation, in making the point that Christian religion was widely available to slaves, said "everyone able to go about, can hear preaching once in two weeks, or once in a month at farthest."

In the cities, too, churchgoing by whites was always rather optional. A British traveler said of New Orleans in 1830: "The people spend the Sunday more in amusements and in shopping (for the shops are generally open on Sunday), than in the walls of their churches."

Often the slaveowners encouraged Christian religious practices, as in this account by a former slave of her baptism on the banks of a pond by the mill, as a teen, and the presence of her owner, Miss Bessie: "A crowd was to be baptized at 2:30 o'clock that evening. The sun was good and hot. I went with my folks. Miss

Bessie went and all the white folks went to see their negroes go under."

It is a dismal thing, nevertheless, to read slave narratives and to note the frequency with which Christian teachings were a repetitive series of Biblical admonishments that a slave must accept his or her lot. Most Christian teachings to slaves were just an extension of farm management.

Yet, there were more bizarre Christian beliefs. A black preacher told a visitor that "we must bear our fate; but in a future world we shall be white men and free." The visitor to the slave state of Missouri had an additional, corrosive memory. "A German whom I met here told me that the blacks believe the damned among the negroes to become monkeys; but if in this shape they behave well, they are advanced to the state of a negro again, and bliss is eventually possible to them, consisting in their turning white, becoming winged, and so on. Whether such ideas are fostered by the Christian clergy I do not know, but I am almost inclined to this opinion."

In fact, often the "proprietors" calmly concluded that "religion was of great importance in the management of slaves." This was regarded as plainly evident after 1830; as a pro-slavery tract said, "[t]he most devout of our slaves are the most faithful and honest in the discharge of their duties to their Masters." A pro-slavery survey of missionary activities among the slaves, written in 1850, quoted an old slave talking to a white preacher: the preaching of the missionaries "had saved more rice for massa than all the locks and keys on the plantation."

VIII. Searches and Punishments by Patrollers

Who knows what unwritten laws were enforced by the patrols against free blacks in the towns and cities? In 1850's Charleston, for example, a survey of Southern laws against free blacks at the time said, "[a] free coloured man must not carry a cane, and his wife is not allowed to wear a veil. Should they walk out together in the street, she must not take his arm; that would be regarded as an act of flagrant impertinence. If they meet a white person, and the path is narrow, they must go aside into the gutter to give unobstructed passage to a white."

In the great solitude of the countryside, too, the patrols had more mandates than ever.

The overall purpose of searches of the slave cabins, garden plots and chicken yards was open and notorious. "The principal object of such visits is to terrify the slaves, and thus secure their good behavior, and especially to prevent their wandering about at night." The cabins were no place of sanctuary. If the search was just for passes or missing slaves, then the cabin would be surrounded by patrollers, and the slaves told to come out one by one with their passes. Or, the patrols just walked into the cabins at night, recalled Ida Henry. "The patrollers would walk through de quarters and homes of de slaves all times of night wid pine torch lights." Sallie Carder's memory: "The patrollers would go about in the quarters at night to see if any of the slaves was out or slipped off. As we sleep on the dirt floors on pallets, the patrollers would walk all over and on us and if we even grunt dey would whip us." It might not matter if a slave violated any rules, recalled Hattie Sugg. "I was at a quiltin' one night when de patrollers come. [Slaves] begin buckin' an jumpin' out de windows. Dey whipped Aunt Jane. I 'member they made her pull her clothes down to her waist. Dey said when dey come up: 'We come to whip you [slaves] pass or no pass.'"

The patrols used the element of surprise when searching a slave cabin. If slave women were sitting around and weaving cloth at night, "all at once here come them paddyrollers, some at the front door and some at the back door." At least one patroller would be placed outside the cabin: this might be "the captain of the company, whose business it was to guard the outside of the house, and see that none of the inmates left." The outsides of the cabins, or huts, have been described this way: "No attempt at any drainage or any convenience existed near them. Heaps of oyster shells, broken crockery, old shoes, rags and feathers were found near each hut. The huts were all alike windowless." Another description:

> We lodged in log huts, and on the bare
> ground. Wooden floors were an
> unknown luxury. In a single room were
> huddled, like cattle, ten or a dozen
> persons, men, women and children. [. .
> .] Our beds were collections of straw and
> old rags, thrown down in corners and
> boxed in with boards. The wind whistled
> and the rain snow blew in through the
> cracks, and the damp earth soaked in
> the moisture till the floor was as miry as
> a pig-sty.

Harriet Jacobs described a search of her cabin in the still widely-read book, *Incidents in the Life of a Slave Girl*, and noted that a patrol "was a grand opportunity for the low whites, who had no negroes of their own to scourge." She reported that "every box, trunk, closet and corner underwent a thorough examination"; the patrollers were surprised to find jars of preserves. Once, when the patrollers found "a bit of writing" - handwritten poems - the patrollers exclaimed: "this here yellow gal's got letters!"

It was an everyday observation that the patrols performed their duties while drunk, "whiling away their time with the help of a fiddle and a bottle of whiskey." It was also an ancient observation. South Carolina's patrol law of 1740 said: "Many irregularities have been committed by former patrols arising chiefly from their drinking too much liquor before or during the time of their riding on duty." In 1759, Georgia's law against drunkenness on patrol in Savannah was passed. "Often have I known a company of licentious and inebriated young men sally forth after an evening's carousal, and in the stillness of night commence their round of domiciliary visits to the quarters of the negroes, while their inmates were buried in sleep."

Also, the patrollers were not all that reliable. A county militia commander in North Carolina, in the midst of the Turner-enhanced heat of the late summer of 1831, wrote to the governor about the patrollers. He wrote: "There are many in this County who are quite refractory & scarcely can be brought to do their turn of service and their pleas are that it is uncertain whether they shall get their pay for their service & that they have no slaves of their own & therefore ought not to be interrupted about the slaves of others."

One need not guess what words were shouted by the patrols as they invaded a cabin. During the earlier periods of the laws regarding slaves, state laws mandated the mutilation of runaway slaves who had been caught; for example, South Carolina's law mandated that the nose of the slave be slit; a fourth offense meant mandatory castration, branding, and loss of an ear. Mutilation either as punishment given by the slaveowner for running away or as a form of identification in case the slave ran away, was called "cropping," and the styles included loss of an ear, or quite commonly, the removal of one or two front teeth. The memoirs are matter of fact on this subject: "a strong and sound tooth was extracted, to serve as a mark to describe her in the case of escape." A pro-slavery book, published a half-century after the Civil War ended, tells us what words were shouted at slaves; it noted gently that the laws requiring mutilation "were sometimes held up by the patrol as a terror to the slave."

Another punishment for running away was to affix a collar with rods of metal, like a birdcage, with a padlock at the back, to a band of metal around or above the forehead, on which hung one or more bells, or from which rods were attached extending into the air, on which hung the bells. The contraption hung one or two feet over the head. "This is not by any means an uncommon punishment," a Georgian former slave recounted. "I have seen many slaves wearing them." The weight of the contraption hurt when stooping to work; sleep was impossible unless crouching. Sometimes there was only one bell: a "common cow bell," as a Northerner recounted after a tour of six Southern states. The same author said that the upper edge of the metal collar "is sometimes serrated, like a saw. Whenever the slave turns his head, the collar chafes his neck. This author did not think that the bells (or bell) were "often applied," as he "was obliged to travel fourteen miles to see one." Naturally, the bells were a convenience and a blessing to the patrols.

Charles Ball, in his memoirs of his years as slave, recounted a story. Ball was in the swamps, miles from his plantation, looking for turtles and turtle eggs on a Sunday. Ball heard an odd sound - "I heard the sound of bells, like those which waggoners place on their horses' shoulders." Ball came upon an escaped slave, with three bells suspended on a metal contraption over his head, and the sight so scared Ball that he started praying out loud. The escaped slave spoke with Ball; he was from the Congo; had been a slave for five years; and had been eating raw turtle eggs, but no turtles, because the sound of the bells scared off the turtles. Ball told him that he would return the following Sunday with a file to remove the contraption. Ball returned the following Sunday, but the escaped slave had hung himself from a tree, with bells on, which scared off the buzzards. Ball's owner was told, and the body was left hanging on the tree, a warning of bone and iron, in a well-known key.

IX. Forms Of Resistance by the Slaves

A. Real-World Punishments for Slaves Secretly Learning to Read or Write and Examples of Resistance

Even a common funeral dirge, sung at the nighttime or Sunday burials of slaves, talked of reading, one day, in the afterlife:

When I can read my title clear

To mansions in the skies,

I bid farewell to every fear

And wipe my weeping eyes.

It was dangerous to learn to read; reading was a "seditious skill." Ann Maria Green said of her slave-life in Maryland, that "to see you with a book in your hand they would almost cut your throat." Carrie Davis said of her slave-life in Alabama: "Us couldn't leave de plantation without a pass; and you better not let 'em catch you wid a book."

Former Alabama slave William Henry Towns recalled the rules about learning to read and write. "Talk 'bout learnin' to read an' write - why, if we so much as spoke of learnin' to read an' 'rite we was scolded like de devil. If we was caught lookin' in a book we was treated same as if we had killed somebody. A servant bett'nt be caught lookin' in a book; didn't make no diff'ence if you wan't doin' nothin' but lookin' at the pictures."

Former Alabama slave Lucindy Lawrence Jurdon recalled, "[u]s never did learn nothing. If us tried to read or write dey would whack our forefingers off." Her memory is similar to George Young's, who was also a former slave from Alabama. "If they catch us l'arnin' to read an' write, they cut us han' off. They didn't 'low us to go to church, neither. Sometimes us slip off an' have a little prayer meetin' by ourselves in a old house with a dirt floor."

An interviewer recorded the memories of James Lucas, a former Mississippi slave. "His master bought eight slaves from Baltimore and some from Virginia. Those that came from Baltimore were sent back as they could read and write and were too smart. His master hung the best slave he had for trying to teach the others how to spell." Alex McCinney testified, "We wasn't 'lowed to read nothin'. I heard ole Marsa tell 'em if they was caught with any books it was a hundred licks." Solomon Northrup was bought by a man named Epps: "Soon after he purchased me, Epps asked me if I could write and read, and on being informed that I had received some instruction in those branches of education, he assured me, with emphasis, if he ever caught me with a book, or with a pen and ink, he would give me a hundred lashes. He said he wanted me to understand that he bought 'niggers' to work and not to educate."

The stouthearted Susie King Taylor was born a slave in Georgia in 1848; she later served in a black regiment of the U.S Army during the Civil War and wrote a book about it. She was raised, along with her brother, by her grandmother, a free woman, in Savannah. Her grandmother sent Susie and her brother to learn to read and write at the home, a half mile away, of a nearby widow, a free black woman. "We went every day about nine o'clock, with our books wrapped in paper to prevent the police or white persons from seeing them."

Thomas H. Jones, a former slave in Wilmington, North Carolina, recounted how he had learned to read, after getting ahold of a spelling book while he worked in town at his master's store. Thomas Jones hid the spelling book under a liquor barrel in his owner's smokehouse; he had a friend named Jacob who taught him to read.

> Jacob next set me a copy which he called pot hooks; then, the letters of the alphabet. These letters were also in my new spelling-book, and according to Jacob's directions, I set them before me for a copy, and wrote on these exercises till I could form all the letters and call them by name. One evening I wrote out my name in large letters - THOMAS JONES.

You could just head for the hills and learn to read, recalled Reverend W.E. Northcross, a former slave.

> At this time I did not know "A" from "B," but I met a man who could read a little. This man liked me and promised to teach me how to read, provided I would keep it a secret. This I gladly promised

to do. [. . .] I secured a blue-back speller and went out on the mountain every Sunday to meet this gentleman, to be taught. I would stay on the mountain all day Sunday without food. I continued this way for a year and succeeded well. I hired my own time and with my blue-back speller went to the mountain to have this man teach me. The mountain was the great school which I attended.

Reverend Northcross's owner found out that he had a blue-back speller. "[H]e simply told me that he heard that I had a book, and if I was caught with it I would be hung."

The testimony of those slaves who learned to read persistently mention Webster's blue-back speller. Webster's spelling book was a chief tool of slave resistance to anti-literacy laws and attitudes. Jenny Proctor, a former slave, recalled: "None of us was 'lowed to see a book or try to learn. They say we git smarter than they was if we learn anything, but we slips around and gits hold of that Webster's old blue-back speller and we hides it till 'way in the night and then we lights a little pine torch, and studies that spelling book. We learn it too. I can now read some now and write a little too."

White children often taught slaves how to read or write, even if no chalk or slate was at hand. A former slave in North Carolina, John C. Becton, recalled how he learned to read. "When the white children studied their lessons I studied with them. When they wrote in the sand I wrote in the sand too. The white children, and not the marster or mistress, is where I got started in learnin' to read or write."

Elijah Marrs, born a slave in Kentucky, and who later became a well-known Baptist preacher, was also taught to read by white children.

> I sought the aid of the white boys, who did all they could in teaching me. They did not know that it was dangerous for a slave to read and write. I availed myself of every opportunity, daily I carried my book in my pocket, and every chance that offered would be learning my A, B, C's. Soon I learned to read. After this the white people would send me daily to the post-office, at

Simpsonville, Ky., a distance of two miles, when I would read the address of the letters; I also would read the newspapers the best I could. There was an old colored man on the place by the name of Ham Graves, who opened a night school, beginning at 10 o'clock at night. I attended his school one year and learned how to write my name and read writing. On every gate-post around the stable, as on the plow handles, you could see where I had been trying to write.

Sam Johnson was a slave preacher and butler on a South Carolina plantation, where the master's young son taught him to read on the sly. The son, forbidden by his parents to drink his favored tea and coffee, got both as payment for lessons in reading and writing. The lessons led to Sam Johnson's ability to read the Bible.

A former slave from Virginia, Peter Randolph, emancipated in 1845 by his master's will, along with 80 other slaves, later, as a pastor in Boston, wrote a book. He wrote, "I was owned, with eighty-one others, by a man named Edlow, and among them all, only myself could either read or write." Peter Randolph had a Christian religious experience at age 11; he then wanted to become a preacher, and thought so for seven years.

> [B]ut then I could not read the Bible, and I thought that I could never preach unless I learned to read the Bible, but I had no one to teach me how to read. A friend showed me the letters, and how to spell words of three letters. [. . .] I used to go to church to hear the white preacher. When I heard him read his text, I would read mine when I got home. Thus did I labor eleven years. [. . .] Then I learned to write. Here I had no teaching; but I obtained a book with the writing alphabet in it, and copied the letters until I could write. I had no slate, so I used to write on the ground. All by myself I learned the art of writing. Then I used to do my own letter-writing, and write my own passes. [. . .] I could do my own writing, unbeknownst to the overseer, and carry my own pass.

Or, perhaps a young slave woman might overhear the master's attempt at secrecy, and get someone else to spell it out. "I couldn't read, but my uncle could," said Elizabeth Batume. "I was a waiting-maid, an' used to help missis to dress in the morning. If massa wanted to tell her something he didn't want me to know, he used to spell it out. I could remember the letters, an' as soon as I got away I ran to uncle an' spelled them over to him, an' he told me what they meant."

Slave preachers were quite rare on the plantations; preaching was helped along by the scarce ability to read the Bible. Slave preachers were not always literate; but many were. Indeed, literacy elevated men to the status of preacher. "Some few slaves could read and write, and dem what could read was most allus called on by de others for preachin'."

There was always an old-fashioned method in learning to read. An interviewer of former slave Mary Gladdy of Georgia in the 1930's wrote this: "Mary Gladdy claims to have never attended school or been privately taught in her life. And she can't write or even form the letters of the alphabet, but she gave her interviewer a very convincing demonstration of her ability to read. When asked how she mastered the art of reading, she replied: 'The Lord revealed it to me.'"

B. The Danger of Prayer and Prayer as Resistance

Much of slave religion was practiced in secret, and these were daily acts of resistance to the laws, the patrols and the slaveholders. Anderson Edwards became a preacher after his days as a slave; he recalled, "We didn't have no song books and the Lord done give us our songs and when we sing them at night it just whispering so nobody hear us."

It could be dangerous for a slave to pray.

Praying was dangerous in Oklahoma. Ida Henry's mother was whipped. "The patrollers wouldn't allow de slaves to hold night services, and one night they caught my mother out praying. They stripped her naked and tied her hands together and wid a rope tied to de handcuffs and threw one end of the rope over a limb and tied de other end to [the] saddle on a horse. As my mother weighed 'bout 200, they pulled her up so that her toes could barely touch de ground and whipped her."

The patrols were prowling the countryside. A memory of Mississippi: "We had no church to go to, but sometimes at night afte' the white folks were asleep, some of the slaves would hide down under the hill an' sing an' pray for de Lord to come an' free 'em. Sometimes slaves from other plantations would come an' sing an' pray with us, but the slaves always had to carry a li'l piece of paper to keep the patterroller from gittin' him."

Praying for freedom was dangerous; here's a memory of former slave Mingo White.

> I remember once ol' Ned White was caught prayin'. The drivers took him the nex' day an' carried him to de pegs, what was four stakes drove in de ground. Ned was made to pull off ever'thang but his pants and lay on his stomach between the pegs while somebody strapped his legs an' arms to the pegs. Them they whupped him until the blood run from him like he was a hog.

You could pray or howl silently into a pot. "There was no churches for slaves, but at nights they would slip off and git in ditches and sing and pray, and when they would sometimes be caught at it they would be whipped. Some of de slaves would turn down big pots and put their heads in them and pray," recalled Sally Carder. You could pray into the earth. "They would dig holes in the ground too, and lie down when they prayed," recalled former slave James Southall.

A memory of the consolations of whispering: "We didn't have no song books and the Lord done give us our songs and when we sing them at night it jus' whispering so nobody hear us." Richard Caruthers, a former slave, recounted how you would deal with a fellow slave whose prayers got too loud.

> Us [slaves] used to have a prayin' ground down in the hollow and sometime we come out of the field . . . scorchin' and burnin' up with nothin' to eat, and we wants to ask the good Lawd to have mercy. [. . .] We takes a pine torch . . . and goes down in the hollow to pray. Some gits so joyous they starts to holler loud and we has to stop up they mouth.

The sounds of the prayers and songs of the slaves were deadened, by them, with wet quilts and rags in muffled, mournful ceremonies. Outdoors, prayer meetings were held at "hush harbors" - woods and thickets - or at a "prayin' ground down in the hollow."

Secret prayers for freedom were constant. "My master used to ask us children, 'Do you folks pray at night?' We said 'No' cause our folks had told us what to say. But the Lord have mercy, there was plenty of that going on. They'd pray, 'Lord, deliver us from under bondage.'"

C. Physical Resistance to the Patrols

Slave patrols were often resisted physically, despite the immediate threat to self-preservation - in the most extreme case, by fighting the patrollers to the death, but this was unusual. In one instance, a patrol came upon a large dance of slaves on Easter night. Twenty-five male slaves fought hand-to-hand with the patrol, resulting in the deaths of two patrollers and six slaves.

A classic method: "Sometimes they fought their way out of their meeting places or threw hot coals in the faces of the intruders." A former slave recalled that a dance at a mill was surrounded by a patrol; those slaves with passes were told to leave. The remaining slaves were told to remove their shirts; one slave "got a shovel and threw fire coals, one shovelful after another, at the patrols. The lights had been extinguished; some of them got burnt in the face and neck badly, while others got clothing burnt. This cleared the way, and the Negroes, even the woman, escaped."

Or coals could be tossed on the floor. Or ashes could be tossed in the faces of the patrol members at a slave cabin door, and the slaves would make a run for it. Of course, fighting and then running was the most common method of in-person physical resistance: "Sometimes a stout man will fight his way through."

There were more severe methods of dealing with the patrols. One method of slave resistance to the patrols, who were local men, was to burn down their homes and property. The North Carolina legislature was petitioned in 1830 by whites from four eastern North Carolina counties to replace the patrols with the county militia. The reason: "The patrols are of no use on account of the danger they subject themselves to." Two patrolmen had "their dwelling houses and other houses burnt down" and a third had his "fodder stack burned." In Princess Anne County, West Virginia, in

1852, an extra patrol was sent out on a Sunday night. A newspaper reported:

> On Sunday night last, this patrol made a descent upon a church where a large number of negroes had congregated for the purpose of holding a meeting, and dispersed them. In a short time, the fodder stacks [piles of corn stalks and leaves] of one of the party who lived near were discovered on fire. The patrol immediately started for the fire, but before reaching the scene it was discovered that the stacks of the other neighbors had shared a like fate, all having no doubt been fired by the negroes for revenge. A strict watch is now kept over them, and most rigid means to make everyone know and keep his place.

Often, slaves set fire to barrels of pitch or tar kilns or turpentine; these acts were so common that the arson laws of the time addressed these acts directly.

Another method of resisting the patrols was to hamper their traveling efficiency by messing with their horses. "The patrollers became so desperate that the colored people cut off their horses' tails and saddle skirts." This was recalled in Missouri: "Uncle Peter Clay of Liberty claims that the young slaves took great delight in docking the tails of the horses of the patrol and tripping them at night by means of ropes stretched across the roads." One tactic was to place grapevines across the road so that the horses of the patrols would tumble. Horses, and even patrol members, could be killed if the grapevine-trap worked. "The plan was this, to get in a ravine and stretch wild grape vines across the road where they knew the patrollers were sure to come. Then they would get on an elevation and commence to sing comic songs. When they would discover them they would start on the run. The patrollers came in contact with the vines and it would knock them off, injuring many of them."

A former slave recounted using clothes lines: "I have known slaves to stretch clothes lines across the street, high enough to let the horse pass, but not the rider; then the boys would run, and the patrols in full chase would be thrown off by running against the lines."

On the roads, of course, you could always just run from the horse-riding patrollers. "Patter-rollers carried a crooked handle-stick which they would try to fasten around the slaves' necks or arms. However, the slaves soon learned that the patter-rollers stick would slide off their bare arms and backs, so they left their shirts if planning to make a visit without a pass."

If the slaves prayed loud enough, the patrols would hear them. One method of keeping the noise down was to place a "big iron pot at the door" to "keep the sound from goin' out." Another method was to pray around a tub of water, because the tub "would catch your voice." If there was a prayer meeting: "There always was a watcher to look out for patty-rollers. They turn a pot down so as not to let the sound go far." Or use the pot this way: "For fear the Patroller would hear 'em they'd put their faces down in a dinner pot."

At a large gathering, such as a dance to which slaves from several plantations were invited, lookouts or scouts were employed to watch for the patrols. It made sense, then, that slaves were forbidden to own their own dogs, who would provide a warning to them. Charleston's ordinance said that blacks could not own dogs, but could possess them, provided the dog had a collar "with the name of some creditable white person" attached. Mississippi, in 1822, authorized patrols to kill all dogs kept by a slave.

Warnings from other slaves that the patrols were nearby were common. Singing could provide a warning that the 'paddyrollers' were around; just call the patrol a rolling pin:

> Old Bill Rolling Pin
>
> He's up the road
>
> And back again
>
> With big eyes, big ears
>
> And a double chin.

Holding a prayer meeting in a secret location was a favored method of hiding from the patrols. "Not being allowed to hold meetings on the plantation, the slaves assemble in the swamps, out of reach of the patrols. They have an understanding among themselves of the time and place of getting together. This is often done by the first one arriving breaking boughs from the trees, and bending them in the direction of the selected spot."

False passes could easily trick illiterate patrollers. The slaves would pick up a piece of a letter and "palm it off" as a pass; another method was to take a real pass and change the dates.

To avoid the patrols at night, one method was to know the habits of the patrols, especially those hours of the night when the patrollers grew sleepy or drunk, or both: "From dark until ten or eleven o'clock at night, the patrols are watchful, and always traversing the country in search of negroes, but towards midnight theses gentlemen grow cold, or sleepy, or weary, and generally betake themselves to some house, where they can procure a comfortable fire."

The pass-less slave could run back to his owner's property or 'dodge' the patrol. To deal with this, laws were passed allowing landowners to punish slaves who had not taken "the most usual and accustomed road." To avoid the patrol when out without a pass, the slave might try to confuse the bloodhounds by hiding in a stream, "dodging in the swamps," or crossing the creeks. Confusing the hounds (working "the conjure" on the hounds, in Henry Green's words) included rubbing turpentine on the feet or hands, rubbing dirt on them, or walking along with an animal, such as a calf.

You could always confuse the hounds and annoy their sensitive noses. A woman from Louisiana recalled: "The colored people said Sam greased his feet with rabbit-grease, and that kept the dogs from him." One former slave described putting red pepper on his feet to throw off the hounds. Slaves might carry "plenty pepper with them to rub on the bottom of their feet at nights when they slipped off so that the dogs couldn't scent them." Another former slave recounted: "We had taken the precaution to bring with us some red onions and spruce pine for the purpose of rubbing our boots so as to divert the scent of the dogs." A Georgian slave had his own method of deterring the hounds. "When other resources failed he would jump into a bed of jameson weeds, and rub the leaves all over his body; for this plant would put him in the condition like that of the Irish-man's skunk, that was said to 'stink so that no man on earth can sell him.'"

Endnotes

I. Introduction

"a million men, women and children": Ira Berlin, *Generations of Captivity: A History of African-American Slaves* (Belknap Press: 2004), p. 161. Print.

Louisiana, two thirds of the slaves were male: Berlin, *Generations of Captivity: A History of African-American Slaves,* pp. 179-180.

free blacks never more than two or three percent: Winthrop D. Jordan, *White over Black: American Attitudes toward the Negro, 1550-1812* (Univ. of North Carolina Press: 1968). Print, p. 407.

II. The Pass, the Patrol, the Power to Whip

The most comprehensive and scholarly study of the slave patrols is Sally E. Hadden, *Slave Patrols: Law and Violence in Virginia and the Carolinas* (Harvard Univ. Press: 2001).

A. Overview.

"dared to be seen talking together": Harriet Ann Jacobs, *Incidents in the Life of a Slave Girl* (Oxford Univ.: 1990) ("Incidents"), p. 99. Print.

"passed in Virginia in 1680": Thomas D. Morris, *Southern Slavery and the Law, 1619-1860* (Chapel Hill: Univ. of North Carolina: 1996), p. 338. Print.

North Carolina, 1715: John Spencer Bassett, *Slavery and Servitude in the Colony of North Carolina* (Baltimore, 1896), pp. 32-33. Archive.org.

"duty of all whites to apprehend such slaves": H. M. Henry, *The Police Control of the Slave in South Carolina* (Emory, VA: 1914), p. 31. Archive.org.

"empowered to correct": Edward, McCrady, *Slavery in the Province of South Carolina, 1670-1770* (Washington D.C.: 1896), p. 647. Archive.org.

Rape: "illicit connection" in Virginia: Robert Sutcliff, *Travels in Some Parts of North America* (York: 1811), p. 53. Archive.org.

"South Carolina did so in 1740": John B. O'Neall, *The Negro Law of South Carolina* (Columbia, 1848), p. 29.

"60 members": Richard C. Wade, *Slavery in the Cities: 1820-1860* (Oxford Univ. Press: 1980), p. 99.

"Resistance was foolish" and "out of place": *Id.*, p. 183; p. 188.

"if found in the streets without a passport after the evening 'gunfire'": Frederick Law Olmsted, *A Journey in the Back Country: (Our Slave States)* (Macon Brothers: 1860), p. 444. Google Books.

B. The Laws of Tennessee as an Example of a Slave Code

"Lordy Honey!" and "waitin' to run 'em down and beat 'em up": Alice Green, Georgia Slave Narratives.

"seemed like stealing": Josiah Henson, *Father Henson's Story of His Own Life* (Boston: 1858) (Amazon, ISBN 9781545136225), p. 19. Print.

"bare back": William Littell and Jacob Swigert, *A Digest of the Statute Law of Kentucky: Being a Collection of All the Acts of the General Assembly, of a Public and Permanent Nature, from the Commencement of the Government to May Session, 1822, Also, the English and Virginia Statutes, Yet in Force; Together with Several Acts of Congress* (Frankfort: Printed by Kendall and Russell, Printers for the State: 1822), p. 981. Google Books.

"travel on the high road": *Compilation of the Public Acts of the Legislative Council of the Territory of Florida*, 1839, p. 225. Google Books.

"Arkansas passed the identical law in 1825": John Steele and James M'Campbell, *Laws of Arkansas Territory* (Little Rock: 1835), p. 531. Google Books.

C. Examples of City Ordinances and County Laws

"seven grown negroes": *Digest of the Ordinances of the City Council of Charleston, from the Year 1783 to July 1818 to Which Are Annexed, Extracts from the Acts of the Legislature Which Relate to the City of Charleston* (Charleston: 1818) ("Charleston Digest") p. 180. Google Books.

"on some visible part of his or her dress": *Charleston Digest*, pp. 185-186.

"marks upon their persons are minutely described": Frederick Law Olmsted, *The Cotton Kingdom: A Traveler's Observations on Cotton and Slavery in the American Slave States* (New York: Mason Brothers, 1861) ("The Cotton Kingdom"), p. 146. Google Books.

"indecent song": *Charleston Digest*, p. 189.

Swimming: Various Authors, *Unchained - Powerful & Unflinching Narratives of Former Slaves: 28 True Life Stories in One Volume* (Kindle Edition) ("Various Authors"). Solomon Northrup, *12 Years a Slave*.

City of Augusta: Ordinances of City of Augusta, 1862.

"so innocent a matter": Various Authors. *Narrative of the Life of Moses Grandy, a Slave in the United States of America*.

"home and orderly": Jeffrey R. Brackett, *The Negro in Maryland* (Baltimore, 1889), p. 110. Archive.org.

"Well, boy": *Id.*, p. 184.

"negroes do not congregate": William Chambers, *American Slavery and Colour* (London: 1857), pp. 205-206. Archive.org.

"a system of espionage": Edward Ingle, *Southern Sidelights* (Boston: 1896), p. 26.

"mechanics, overseers": Kate Pickard, *The Kidnapped and the Ransomed, Being the Personal Recollections of Peter Still and His Wife Vina after Forty Years of Slavery* (Syracuse: 1856) ("Kidnapped"), p. 160. Archive.org.

"clatter of horses' hoofs": Northrup, *12 Years a Slave*.

"'carrying 'great big torches of fire'": Mom Ryer Emmanuel. South Carolina Slave Narratives.

Martha Jackson and Carrie Davis: Alabama Slave Narratives.

"hunted her with dogs": Quoted in Elizabeth Fox-Genovese, *Within the Plantation Household: Black and White Women of The Old South* (Univ. of North Carolina: 2006), p. 321. Print.

"traversing the streets with cowskins": Theodore Dwight Weld, *American Slavery As It Is: Testimony of a Thousand Witnesses* (New York: American Anti-Slavery Society, 1839), p. 64. Google Books.

"a repose and security known nowhere else": William Harper, James Henry Hammond, William Gilmore

Simms, Thomas R. Dew, *The Pro-slavery Argument; as Maintained by the Most Distinguished Writers of the Southern States* (Phil.: 1853), p. 111. Google Books.

"requiring all citizens to help the patrols if called upon": Trexler, *Slavery in Missouri,* p. 183.

"Their safety depends upon their vigilance": Frederick Douglass, *My Bondage and My Freedom* (Univ. of Illinois: 1987), p. 169. Print.

"Jump along Jericho": William Francis Allen, Charles Pickard Ware and Lucy McKim Garrison, *Slave Songs of the United States* (New York: 1871), p. 35. Google Books.

"some other way by which they may know the hour when to be at home": Weld, *Testimony of a Thousand Witnesses,* p. 22 (narrative of Sarah M. Grimke).

III. The Hardening of Slavery after 1830: The Reaction Takes Hold

A. The Profitability of Cotton Gives Rise to the Slave Power

Haiti: *See* Robin Blackburn, *The Overthrow of Colonial Slavery: 1776-1848* (Verso: 2011), Chapter 6,

"Revolutionary Emancipationism and the Birth of Haiti." Print.

"No black man ought to be permitted to turn a Preacher": Nicholas May, "Holy Rebellion: Religious Assembly Laws in Antebellum South Carolina and Virginia," *The American Journal of Legal History* 49, no. 3 (2007): 237-56. *JSTOR*, http://www.jstor.org/stable/25664424.

"an almost-doubling of the price of slaves": Edward E. Baptist, *The Half Has Never Been Told: Slavery and the Making of American Capitalism* (Basic: 2014), p. 174. Print.

"the price of slaves nearly tripled": U.B. Phillips, "The Slave Labor Problem in the Charleston District." *Political Science Quarterly*, Vol. 22, no. 3 (1907), pp. 416–439; p. 436. *JSTOR*, www.jstor.org/stable/2141056.

"stress on clock time": Robin Blackburn, *The American Crucible: Slavery, Emancipation and Human Rights* (Verso: 2013), p. 310. Print.

British Parliament: Blackburn, *The Overthrow of Colonial Slavery*, pp. 456-459; Blackburn, *The American Crucible*, p. 281.

"the slave power wrenched from the soil": J. H. Ingraham, *The South-west: By a Yankee*, Vol. II (New York: 1835), p. 91. Archive.org.

"The old rule of pricing a negro": U.B. Phillips, *A Documentary History of American Industrial Society* (Cleveland: 1910), p. 73. Archive.org.

"fully three-fourths of the slave labor was applied to that crop": A.B. Hart, *The American Nation: A History*, Vol. 16, "Slavery and Abolition, 1831-1841" (New York and London: 1906), p. 59. Archive.org.

"westward into the 'back country'": M.B. Hammond, *The Cotton Industry* (New York and London: 1897), p. 43; p. 50. Archive.org.

"women and grown-up girls are usually sold into the cotton-growing States": G.W. Featherstonhaugh, *Excursion through the Slave States* (New York: 1844), p. 38. Archive.org.

"the cultivation of rice thins the black population so fast": Flanders, *Plantation Slavery in Georgia*, p. 185.

Men and women in the towns; traveler diary: Wade, *Slavery in the Cities*, pp. 24-26; pp. 163-164.

"planters often abandoned their fields" and "plan of planting": Hammond, *The Cotton Industry*, pp. 83-84; p. 104.

"shaggy unkempt grounds": Frances Anne Kemble, *Journal of a Residence on a Georgian Plantation* (New York: 1863), p. 236.

"What did you see": Ingle, *Southern Sidelights*, p. 57.

"a single laborer can cultivate": Hammond, *The Cotton Industry*, p. 47.

British traveler: Charles Lyell, *A Second Visit to the United States of North America: In Two Volumes*, Vol. 2 (London: 1850) (*"A Second Visit"*), p. 109. Archive.org.

"thicker than locusts in Egypt": *Southern Advocate*, 8 June 1827, *quoted in* Christopher D. Haveman, "The Removal Of The Creek Indians From The Southeast, 1825-1838," unpublished dissertation (Auburn Univ.: 2009), p. 63.

"colonize a plantation": William Pope Harrison, *The Gospel among the Slaves: A Short Account of Missionary Operations among the African Slaves of the Southern States* (Nashville: 1893), p. 260. Archive.org.

"might travel by flatboat" and "the worst masters": Pickard, *Kidnapped*, p. 144; p. 198.

"growing gang labor farms": Ingle, *Southern Sidelights*, pp. 15-17

"the clank of chained feet marching": W. E. B. DuBois, *The Souls of Black Folks* (Dover Books: 1994), p. 76. Print.

Berlin, *Generations of Captivity, A History of African–American Slaves*, p. 161.

1846 newspaper ad: Lyell, *A Second Visit*, p. 161.

"on the Cahawba" and "4000 to 5000 per annum": Hodgson, Adam Hodgson, *Letters from North America: Written During a Tour in The United States and Canada* (London: 1824), p. 113; p. 194. Archive.org.

B. The Cotton Slaveholders Expand by Taking the Land of the Indians

"To the west, Texas beckoned those small farmers; to the south, Cuba beckoned the big slaveholders, as did Central America": See Frederick Jackson Turner's essays, "The South" and "Colonization of the West," in A.B. Hart, *Social and Economic Forces in American History* (New York and London: 1913). Archive.org.

Governor of Georgia: George R. Gilmer, *Sketches of Some of the First Settlers of Upper Georgia, of The Cherokees, and the Author* (New York: 1855), pp. 468-469; p. 508. Archive.org.

Alabama's "city prices": Joseph G. Baldwin, *The Flush Times of Alabama and Mississippi* (San Francisco: 1876), p. 83; p. 97. Archive.org.

"British visitor in 1846": Lyell, *A Second Visit*, p. 82.

"transferring the Aborigines": *Id.*, p. 33.

"full of deer and turkeys": F.L. Riley ed., *Autobiography of Gideon Lincecum* (Publications of The Mississippi Historical Society: 1904), pp. 443-509. Google Books.

Choctaws of Mississippi: Arthur H. De Rosier, *The Removal of the Choctaw Indians* (Univ. of Tennessee: 1981), p. 87; p. 124; p. 162. Print

"Lively picnics are now held on these ancient Indian mounds": Bremer, *The Homes of the New World*, p. 338.

C. Slaves Replace the Indians; the Forests Are Felled

"Virginia is in fact a negro-raising State for other States": Leonard Bacon, *Slavery Discussed in Occasional Essays, from 1833 to 1846* (New York:1846), p. 78 and p. 94. Archive.org.

German Duke: Duke Karl Bernhard, *Travels through North America During The Years 1825 And 1826* (Phil.: 1828) ("Travels"), p. 18.

Georgia's forests: Jesse Torrey, *A Portraiture of Domestic Slavery in The United States* (Phil.: 1817), pp. 485-487. Archive.org.

"100 million acres were cleared by 1850," techniques and "two hundred acres or so of forest clearing as the labor of a lifetime": Martin L. Primack, "Land

Clearing Under Nineteenth-Century Techniques: Some Preliminary Calculations." *The Journal of Economic History*, Vol. 22, no. 4 (1962), pp. 484–497. *JSTOR*, www.jstor.org/stable/2116108.

"Thirteen days previously this was the middle of a wood, and not a tree was cut down!": Hodgson, *Letters from North America*, p. 40.

"The man's employment I recognised from his whip": Bernhard, *Travels*, pp. 14-15.

"A typical day'"": Flanders, *Plantation Slavery in Georgia*, p. 122.

"Where those wild dances were danced, and their wigwams stood, now stands Macon": Fredrika Bremer, *The Homes of the New World* (New York: 1853), p. 322. Archive.org.

D. The Churches Cave to the Slave Power

"Before 1830 the South had hundreds of antislavery organizations with thousands of members": Elizabeth Fox-Genovese and Eugene D. Genovese, *The Mind of the Master Class: History and Faith in the Southern Slaveholders' Worldview* (Cambridge Univ. Press: 2005), p. 231. Print.

"traces of an all-wise Providence": William S. Drewry, *Slave Insurrections in Virginia (1830-1865)* (Wash. D.C.: 1900), p. 184. Archive.org.

Kentucky: Asa Earl Martin, *The Anti-slavery Movement in Kentucky, Prior to 1850* (Louisville: 1918), p. 80. Google Books.

"Quakers and the breakaway Wesleyan Methodists": Fox-Genovese and Genovese, *The Mind of the Master Class*, pp. 234-237.

"Proslaveryism had become the prevailing sentiment in both Church and state." John H. Caldwell, *Slavery and Southern Methodism* (Newman, Ga.: 1865), p. 72. Archive.org.

"the decline in the revival" due to abolitionists: Harrison, *The Gospel among the Slaves*, p. 94.

IV. Fear of Insurrection Haunts the South after 1830

A. A Plot for Slave Insurrection Is Discovered in Camden, South Carolina in 1816

Camden plot - "one a class leader": L. Glen Inabinet, "The July Fourth Incident of 1816: An Insurrection Plotted by Slaves in Camden, South Carolina," *South Carolina Legal History*, ed. Herbert A. Johnson (Univ. of S. Carolina: 1980), pp. 209-221.

B. The Vesey Plot Is Discovered in Charleston, South Carolina in 1822

"[b]orn a conjurer" and "elude the patrol": Thomas Wentworth Higginson, "The Story of Denmark Vesey," *The Atlantic* (June 1861).

"every pamphlet he could lay his hands on": James Hamilton, *Negro Plot: An Account of the Late Intended Insurrection among a Portion of the Blacks of the City of Charleston, South Carolina, Published by the Authority of the Corporation of Charleston* (Boston: 1822). Archive.org.

"250 pike heads": Herbert Aphtheker, *American Negro Slave Revolts* (New York: 1963), p. 272. Archive.org.

"no black mechanics": *Id.*, p.115.

Charleston City Council: *Quoted in* May, *Holy Rebellion*, p. 250.

"dangerous infection of the alphabet": Higginson, *The Story Of Denmark Vesey*.

"the city government demolished the church building": Robert N. Rosen, *A Short History of Charleston* (Univ. of South Carolina: 1999), p. 74. Print.

"slaveowners switched the slaves to white churches" and black churches: Albert J. Raboteau, *Slave*

Religion: The "Invisible Institution" in the Antebellum South (Oxford Univ. Press: 2004), p. 178; p. 188; pp. 200-204; p. 207. Print.

"about 3,000": Aptheker, *American Negro Slave Revolts*, p. 275.

"hopelessness of physical defence": DuBois, *The Souls of Black Folks*, p. 123.

"right to revolt is perfect": Chambers, *American Slavery and Colour*, p. 174.

"27,339 slaves and 4,679 whites": U. B. Phillips, "The Slave Labor Problem in the Charleston District." *Political Science Quarterly*, vol. 22, no. 3 (1907), pp. 416–439. *JSTOR*, www.jstor.org/stable/2141056.

"largest slave marts": Robin Blackburn, *The Making of New World Slavery: From the Baroque to the Modern, 1492-1800* (Verso: 2010), p. 461. Print.

Charleston letter: U. B. Phillips, *Plantation and Frontier Documents: 1649-1863: Illustrative of Industrial History in the Colonial & Ante-bellum South* (Cleveland: 1909), p. 115. Google Books.

"new state law jailed": Rosen, *A Short History of Charleston*, p. 98.

"a certificate from the local court" and Charleston: Henry, *The Police Control of the Slave in South Carolina*, pp. 178-179 and p. 155.

Charleston visitor: Bernard, *Travels*, p. 7.

C. The Reaction to Nat Turner's 1831 Slave Rebellion

"a servile insurrection deserving the name": Drewry, *Slave Insurrections in Virginia*, p. 182.

"bore upon his sword the head of a rebel" and lynching: James E. Cutler, *Lynch-Law* (New York: 1905), p. 94; p. 105; p. 113; p. 122 and p. 124. Archive.org.

D. White Fear after the Nat Turner Insurrection

"headlong to the swamps": Drewry, *Slave Insurrections in Virginia*, p. 179.

season of terror: Aptheker, *American Negro Slave Revolts,* p. 327.

Petitions re hogs and dogs: Drewry, *Slave Insurrections in Virginia*, p. 169.

"lynch club": Cutler, *Lynch-Law*, p. 96, fn. 1.

"deranged from apprehension"; Virginia planter quote and newspaper quote: Aptheker, *American Negro Slave Revolts*, p. 307.

North Carolina's fear: Bassett, *Slavery in the State of North Carolina*, p. 97.

In North Carolina, "It later became a crime to teach slaves to read; that law was opposed by the Quakers": Stephen B. Weeks, *Southern Quakers and Slavery* (Baltimore: 1896), pp. 231-232. Archive.org.

"Free blacks, who had been able to vote since 1776, lost the right to vote": Drewry, *Slave Insurrections in Virginia*, p. 170, footnote 2.

"The patrol was now given large powers of arrest" and North Carolina: Bassett, *Slavery in the State of North Carolina*, pp. 17-19.

Charity Bowery: L. Maria Child, *Letters from New York* (New York: 1845), p. 55. Archive.org.

Governor of Virginia: Barton Haxall Wise, *The Life of Henry A. Wise of Virginia, 1806-1876* (New York: 1899), p. 159. Google Books.

"he cannot sleep soundly at nights": Flanders, *Plantation Slavery in Georgia*, p. 28

Charity Bowery and "Old Prophet Nat": A.B. Hart, *Slavery and Abolition, 1831-1841* (New York and London: 1906), p. 218. Archive.org.

"governor of Virginia wrote a letter in 1831": Letter from Governor John Floyd (Virginia) to Governor James Hamilton (South Carolina), November 19, 1831, published on the web by the Nat Turner Project, available at http://www.natturnerproject.org/gov-floyd-to-gov-hamilton-jr.

V. The Churches Propose Oral Instruction of the Slaves

"blacks were destined to 'the lowest state of servitude, slaves'" and "all efforts to extinguish black slavery are idle": Larry R. Morrison, "The Religious Defense of American Slavery before 1830," *Journal of Religious Thought*, Vol. 37, Issue 2 (1981), p. 16 and p. 18.

A. The Idea of Teaching Religion to the Slaves Is Driven by Northern Criticism "heathenish darkness": Bacon, *Slavery Discussed in Occasional Essays*, p. 60.

"The process is a very ticklish one"; "their cattle" and "lately been ejected": Kemble, *Journal of a Residence on a Georgian Plantation*, p. 72; p. 57; p. 91.

"Divine Law": Raboteau, *Slave Religion*, p. 154. .

"instill principles of rebellion": Harrison, *The Gospel among the Slaves*, p. 150.

"guards, guns and bayonets": Raboteau, *Slave Religion*, p. 164.

B. The Churches Retreat from Opposition to Slavery

Charles Jones, sermon: Charles Colcock Jones, *The Religious Instruction of the Negroes. A Sermon, Delivered Before Associations of Planters in Liberty and M'intosh Counties, Georgia, 1831* (Princeton: 1822) (Forgotten Books: 2017). Print. Charles Colcock Jones, book: *The Religious Instruction of the Negroes in the United States* (Savannah: 1842). Archive.org.

C. The Camp Meeting Movement, a White Revival, Takes off after 1830

"[w]e had no protracted meetings on negro missions": Harrison, *The Gospel among the Slaves*, p. 272.

"From Virginia to Texas, revivals prepared the South to meet the abolitionist offensive": Fox-Genovese and Genovese, *The Mind of the Master Class*, pp. 418-423; p. 515.

"no longer any danger that the professed missionary would become an incendiary": Harrison, *The Gospel among the Slaves*, p. 297.

Fredrika Bremer: Bremer, *The Homes of the New World*, p. 308; p. 311.

the Mississippi pastor: William Channing, *An Inquiry into the History of Slavery, Its Introduction into the United States* (Wash. D.C.: 1841), p. 122. Archive.org.

Kentucky Baptists: J. H. Spencer, *A History of Kentucky Baptists* (Cincinnati, 1886), pp. 673-677, 691-694. Archive.org.

"much whiskey sold": Raboteau, *Slave Religion*, p. 225.

"[m]any remain in the church only a few months": Various Authors. John Dixon Long, *Pictures of Slavery in Church and State*.

D. The Missionary Movement to the Slaves of the Plantations Takes off after 1830

"minimally touched by Christianity": Raboteau, *Slave Religion*, p. 149.

church numbers and church reports: W.E.B. DuBois, *The Negro Church* (Atlanta: 1903), pp. 26-27. Archive.org.

"Methodists took the lead": Raboteau, *Slave Religion*, p. 176.

"increase of only 165," New River, and "well-known sermon": Harrison, *The Gospel among the Slaves*, p. 158; p. 175 and p. 176.

"combat African heathenism": Donald G. Mathews, *Religion in the Old South* (Chicago Univ. Press: 1994), p. 205. Print.

"capable white missionaries": Patterson, *The Negro in Tennessee*, p. 117. "three hundred slaves": Dubois, *The Negro Church*, p. 28.

"310 members" and "over $800" : Heather Rachel White, "'The Glory of Southern Christianity': Methodism and the Mission to the Slaves," *Methodist History*, 39:2, Jan. 2001, pp. 115-116

"class of nearly two hundred"; "214 children"; and "five islands": Harrison, *The Gospel among the Slaves*, p. 162; p. 165; p. 173.

George Moore: Harrison, *The Gospel among the Slaves*, p. 205; p. 199; pp. 206-209; pp. 186-187; p. 117; p. 229. "turbulent slaveholders": Eugene D. Genovese, *Roll, Jordan, Roll: The World the Slaves Made.* (New York: Pantheon, 1974), pp. 186-187; p.

117. Print. This is the seminal work on resistance by the slaves and the world they made within the confines of slavery.

"Intelligence and slavery have no affinity with each other": DuBois, *The Negro Church*, p. 27.

"[e]very Methodist preacher was regarded as an abolitionist agent": Mary Helm, *From Darkness to Light: The Story of Negro Progress* (New York and London: 1909), pp. 62-64. Archive.org

"twenty violins": Lyell, *A Second Visit*, p. 269.

"very angry with them for their love of dancing and music": Bremer, *The Homes of the New World*, p. 290

"19 missionaries": Harrison, *The Gospel among the Slaves*, p. 83.

"ten percent of the 2.7 million slaves were formally Christian": Martin, *The Anti-Slavery Movement in Kentucky Prior To 1850*, p. 79, fn. 3.

"if he was a Methodist, his slaves were Methodists":
I.E. Lowery, *Life on the Old Plantation in
Ante-Bellum Days* (Columbia, S.C.: 1911), p. 144.
Archive.org.

"The first time I was sprinkled": Lucretia Alexander.
Arkansas Slave Narratives.

"a plantation had to take whatever preacher came":
Genovese, *Roll Jordan Roll*, p. 189.

"owners were either Methodists or of no Church
affiliation": Harrison, *The Gospel among the Slaves*,
p. 287.

Baptists in Alabama and Lundsford Lane: DuBois,
The Negro Church, p. 29.

VI. The Slave States Pass Laws to Control the
Expanding Slave Population and Crush
Insurrectionary Ideas and Possibilities

A. The Laws

1. Laws Prohibiting Free Blacks and Slaves From
Learning to Read or Write

Tom Hawkins: Georgia Slave Narratives.

"at nine o'clock a great bell": Drewry, *Slave
Insurrections in Virginia*, p. 175.

Georgia legislature: Massachusetts General Court. Joint Special Committee on Slavery, 1836. Google Books.

Tennessee, 1831: Patterson, *The Negro in Tennessee*, pp. 154-155.

if a "free coloured man travels without passports": John Howard Hinton, *The History and Topography of the United States of North America: From the Earliest Period to the Present Time* (Boston: 1834), p. 328. Archive.org.

"legally permitted by all the colonies" and "Georgia now declared": E. Jennifer Monaghan, "Reading for the Enslaved, Writing for the Free: Reflections on Liberty and Literacy," ["Reading"] *Proceedings of the American Antiquarian Society.* American Antiquarian Society 108:309-341 (October 1998), p. 324; p. 317.

"Every year adds to the number of those who can read and write": Carter Godwin Woodson, *The Education of the Negro Prior to 1861: A History of the Education of the Colored People of the United States from the Beginning of Slavery to the Civil War* (Knickerbocker Press: 1915), p. 157. Archive.org.

Savannah: Monaghan, *Reading*, p. 329.

"a newspaper wrote in 1818": George M. Stroud, *A Sketch of the Laws Relating to Slavery in the Several States of the United States of America* (Philadelphia: 1827), p. 90. Archive.org.

"If a free black was caught doing so, he was fined and whipped - whites faced prison": O'Neall, *The Negro Law of South Carolina*, p. 23.

"Vilest crimes": Various Authors. W. Craft and E Craft, *Running a Thousand Miles for Freedom.*

Jefferson's plantation: Antonio T. Bly, "'Pretends He Can Read': Runaways and Literacy in Colonial America, 1730—1776." *Early American Studies*, Vol. 6, no. 2 (2008), pp. 261–294. *JSTOR*, www.jstor.org/stable/23546575.

Quote from *Southern Literary Messenger*: Wade, *Slavery in the Cities*, p. 91.

Milla Granson: Angela Y. Davis, *Women, Race & Class* (Vintage Books: 1982), p. 251, fn. 58, *quoting* Laura S. Haviland, *A Woman's Life-Work, Labors and Experiences* (Chicago: Publishing Association of Friends, 1889). Print.

Quote about Massa K: Kemble, *Journal of a Residence on a Georgian Plantation,* pp. 271-272.

"Can you believe us to be such unspeakable fools?": Harper, *et al.*, *The Pro-slavery Argument*, p. 124.

"Sixty of his pamphlets": Monaghan, *Reading*, pp. 329-330.

Missouri, 1857: Donnie D. Bellamy, "The Education of Blacks in Missouri Prior to 1861." *The Journal of Negro History*, vol. 59, no. 2, 1974, pp. 143–157. *JSTOR*, www.jstor.org/stable/2717326.

"The tract said": Harper, *et al.*, *The Pro-slavery Argument*, p. 3; pp. 14-15; pp. 36-38; p. 115.

"Our excuse for keeping them in ignorance": Caldwell, *Slavery and Southern Methodism*, pp. 23-24.

"Sabbath-schools are broken up in Kentucky": John Rankin, *Letters on American Slavery: Addressed to Mr. Thomas Rankin, Merchant at Middlebrook, Augusta County, Va. 1793-1886*. (Boston: 1838), pp. 21-22. Archive.org.

"Incendiary pamphlets": *Proceedings of the Citizens of Charleston, on the Incendiary Machinations, Now in Progress against the Peace and Welfare of the Southern States, Published by Order of Council* (Charleston: 1835). Archive.org.

"four hundred slaves rose up": Aptheker, *American Negro Slave Revolts*, p. 333.

"[E]mancipation itself would not satisfy these fanatics": Harper, *et al.*, *The Pro-slavery Argument*, pp. 126-127.

"[d]oes chivalrous South Carolina quail": May, *Holy Rebellion*, pp. 237-56.

"stir up a servile war": Martin, *The Anti-Slavery Movement in Kentucky Prior to 1850*, p. 74, fn. 40.

2. Laws Banning Religious and Other Gatherings of Free Blacks and Slaves

Georgia and Delaware laws: See Woodson's brilliant chapter, "The Reaction," in *The Education of the Negro*.

"nurseries of self-government": Wade, *Slavery in the Cities*, p. 172.

South Carolina laws: *The Statutes at Large of South Carolina*, Vol. 7, Columbia: 1840, pp. 440-441. Google Books.

Pendleton, South Carolina curfew: Henry, *The Police Control of the Slave in South Carolina*, p. 44.

West Tennessee: C. Perry Patterson, *The Negro in Tennessee*, p. 51, fn. 136.

"[n]ot even Nat's confession to Mr. Gray could be sold in the South": Drewry, *Slave Insurrections in Virginia*, p. 169.

"Maryland, in 1831": Brackett, *The Negro in Maryland*, pp. 199-201, pp. 239-241.

"enslaved and sold at public auctions": *Id.*, pp. 176-177; Chambers, *American Slavery and Colour*, p. 187.

"The plain policy of the State": Brackett, *The Negro in Maryland*, p. 181.

"the law was strengthened in 1845" and "10 years in prison": *Id.*, pp. 225-227.

"In 1833, when the stars fell": Katherine E. Rohrer, "Slaveholding Women and the Religious Instruction of Slaves in Post-Emancipation Memory," *Journal of Southern Religion* 15 (2013): http://jsr.fsu.edu/issues/vol15/rohrer.html.

"attendance of about 1459": Woodson, *The Education of the Negro*, p. 185.

3. Laws Banning Abolitionist Writings

Charles Olcott: Charles Olcott, *Two Lectures on the Subjects of Slavery and Abolition: Compiled for the Special Use of Anti-slavery Lecturers and Debaters* (Massillon, Ohio: 1838), p. 38; pp. 43-44. Archive.org.

"observer noted in 1836": E.A. Andrews, *Slavery and the Domestic Slave-trade* (Boston: 1836) p. 159. Archive.org.

"closed oligarchy with a political policy": W.E.B. Dubois, *The Suppression of the African Slave Trade to the United States of America* (New York: 1904), p. 153. Archive.org.

"report in 1837": Thomas Price, *Slavery in America* (London: 1837), p. 78. Google Books.

"containing the speech of J.Q. Adams": John Thompson, *The Life of John Thompson, A Fugitive Slave* (Worchester: 1856), p. 38. Archive.org.

"1854 slave manual": Robert Collins, *Essay on the Treatment and Management of Slaves* (Boston: 1853), p. 14. Archive.org.

B. Slave Religion

"Sometimes us sing and pray all night": *Quoted in* Raboteau, *Slave Religion*, p. 213.

"songs in a whisper and pray in a whisper": Raboteau, *Slave Religion*, p. 214.

"they would want a real meetin' with some real preachin'" and "Three things characterized this religion of the slave,—the Preacher, the Music, and the Frenzy": DuBois, *The Souls of Black Folks,* Chapter 10, "Of the Faith of the Fathers."

"big baptizings": Testimony of Mahalia Jewel, Georgia Slave Narratives, p. 319.

"a black man name Joe": Walter Calloway, Texas Slave Narratives.

"Yes sir! Folks had religion in dem days, the Old Time Religion": Aunt Easter Jackson. Georgia Slave Narratives.

"the old christians sing and pray until four in the morning": Raboteau, *Slave Religion*, p. 222.

Mose Hursey; "They'd shout, 'I got the glory'": Raboteau, *Slave Religion*, p. 221.

"'figurations of the spirit in them days": Raboteau, *Slave Religion*, p. 272.

"ghost lore, witchcraft": Raboteau, *Slave Religion*, p. 275.

Conjurers: Raboteau, *Slave Religion*, p. 283

C. Why Go off the Plantation without a Pass?

Franklin Henry: Henson, *Father Henson's Story of His Own Life*, p. 187.

homemade banjos: Bremer, *The Homes of the New World*, p. 371

"we made our own instruments": Anderson Edwards. Texas Slave Narratives.

"to get my mammy tobacco": Norman R. Yetman, *Voices from Slavery: 100 Authentic Slave Narratives* (Dover Books: 2000), p. 263 (narrative of Henry Cheatam). Print.

"Those that could not show passes were whipped, both the negro girls and boys alike": Henry Clay Morman. Kentucky Slave Narratives.

"Courtin' some gal": Henry Green. Arkansas Slave Narratives.

"patter rolls or no patter rolls": Green Cumby. Texas Slave Narratives.

"husband thus chastised": Andrews, *Slavery and the Domestic Slave-trade*, p. 102.

"slipping out to meet one another at night": Lucy Mccullough. Georgia Slave Narratives.

"Wasn't I a goodlookin' woman?": Louisa Davis. South Carolina Slave Narratives.

"mortifying to be stripped and flogged in the presence of a girl": Thompson, *The Life of John Thompson*, p. 71.

"constantly liable to separation, in the changing of property": Collins, *Essay on the Treatment and Management of Slaves*, p. 12.

"two boys and four girls, were put on a train": Charles Grandison Parson, *Inside View of Slavery, Or, a Tour Among the Planters* (Boston: 1855), p. 119. Archive.org.

"known to physicians as Nostalgia": Olmsted, *The Cotton Kingdom*, p. 124.

D. Examples of Passes

"It has a tendency to make them discontented": Parsons, *Inside View of Slavery*, p. 122.

"I had seen his papers before they were wetted": Yuval Taylor, *I Was Born a Slave: An Anthology of Classic Slave Narratives* (Chicago: 1999), p. 513. Print.

"to give them a written pass to go to town": Samuel Bannister Harding, *Life of George R. Smith, Founder of Sedalia, Mo.* (Sedalia: 1904), p. 49. Google Books.

"sample form": O'Neall, *The Negro Law of South Carolina*, p. 40.

"line up for the roll call": Joseph Kelly Turner and John Luther Bridgers, *History of Edgecombe County, North Carolina* (Raleigh: 1920), pp. 164-165. Google Books.

"the name of John Brown": John Brown and L. A. Chamerovzow, *Slave Life in Georgia: A Narrative of the Life, Sufferings, and Escape of J. Brown, a Fugitive Slave, Now in England* (London: 1855), p. 149. Google Books.

E. What Happened if a Slave Was Caught without a Pass?

"old hen": John Brown, *Slave Life in Georgia*, p. 72.

"fenced in whippin' post": Charley Mitchell. Texas Slave Narratives.

"every time they hit me the blood and hide done fly": Ira Berlin, Marc Favreau and Steven F. Miller, *Remembering Slavery: African Americans Talk About Their Personal Experiences of Slavery and Emancipation* (New York: 1998), p. 172. Narrative of former slave Green Cumby. Print.

"Some received five hundred lashes": Child, *Incidents* p. 98.

"flogged four in a night": Weld, *Testimony of a Thousand Witnesses*, p. 14.

"whipped about fifty that night": Harry Smith, *Fifty Years of Slavery in the United States of America* (Grand Rapids: 1891) ("Fifty Years"), p. 22. Google Books.

"he is very well off if he gets only two hundred": Benjamin Drew, *The Refugee: Or, the Narratives of Fugitive Slaves in Canada* (Boston: 1856), p. 249. Narrative of Philip Younger.

"the drunken caprice of the patrols": Andrews, *Slavery and the Domestic Slave-trade*, p. 102.

"ten with the bull-whip, properly laid on, will cut any man's life out": Brown, *Slave Life in Georgia*, p. 193.

"a lucrative day for the patroller": Various Authors. Solomon Northrup, *Twelve Years a Slave*.

"compelled by the lash to keep up with their speed": Child, *Incidents*, p. 103.

"I saw all of it with my own two eyes": Octavia V. R. Albert, *The House of Bondage, Or, Charlotte Brooks and Other Slaves* (New York: 1891) ("The House of Bondage"), p. 72. Google Books.

"never allowed to see a negro, except while training to catch him": Olmsted, *The Cotton Kingdom*, p. 156.

"carry a gory lash to the master, for a piece of bread": Lewis Garrard Clarke, Milton Clarke, Jonathan Walker and La Roy Sunderland, *Interesting Memoirs and Documents Relating to American Slavery and the Glorious Struggle Now Making for Complete*

Emancipation (London: 1846) ("Interesting Memoirs And Documents"), pp. 87-88. Google Books.

"cruelly scourged for telling lies about white men": Child, *Incidents*, p. 99.

"females fear ever indignity": Andrews, *Slavery and the Domestic Slave-trade*, p. 102.

"power to seize any negro slave": Austin Steward, *Twenty-two Years a Slave, and Forty Years a Freeman: Embracing a Correspondence of Several Years, While President of Wilberforce Colony, London, Canada West* (Rochester: 1857). Google Books.

"robbed of clothing": Child, *Incidents*, pp. 98-99.

F. The Necessity of Illiteracy

"who could not read a guideboard": Clarke *et al.*, *Interesting Memoirs and Documents*, p. 80; p. 28.

"menacing influences": Frederick Douglass, *My Bondage and My Freedom*, p. 275.

"teaching a favorite slave to read": O'Neall, *The Negro Law of South Carolina*, p. 22.

"I had no slate, so I used to write on the ground.": Peter Randolph, *Sketches of Slave Life, Or, Illustrations of the 'Peculiar Institution'* (Boston: 1855), p. 15. Google Books.

"but they forgit it 'fore the next Sunday": W.L. Bost. North Carolina Slave Narratives.

"Alabama, with a maximum of 25 years": Clement Comer Clay, *A Digest of the Laws of the State of Alabama: Containing All the Statutes of a Public and General Nature, in Force at the Close of the Session of the General Assembly, in February, 1843; to Which Are Prefixed, the Declaration of Independence, the Constitution of the United States, the Act to Enable the People of Alabama to Form a Constitution and State Government, &c., and the Constitution of the State of Alabama, with an Appendix, and a Copious Index* (Tuskaloosa: 1843), p. 419. Google Books.

"the slave was sold in two days": Albert, *The House of Bondage*, pp. 109-113.

"The slave must carry back a note to his master": James Stuart, *Three Years in North America* (Edinburgh: 1833), p. 254. Google Books.

"under some liquor barrels": Thomas H. Jones, *The Experience of Thomas Jones Who Was a Slave for Forty-three Years* (Springfield: 1854), p. 15. Google Books.

"and spelled out 'When I Can Read My Title Clear'": Alberto Manguel, *A History of Reading* (Viking: 1996), p. 280. Print. Manguel cites Janet Duitsman Cornelius, *When I Can Read My Title Clear: Literacy, Slavery and Religion in the Antebellum South* (Columbia, S.C.: 1991).

"Henry bought me the Introduction to the English Reader": Thompson, *The Life of John Thompson*, p. 105.

"a letter at a time": James Redpath and John R. McKivigan, *The Roving Editor, Or, Talks with Slaves in the Southern States* (New York: 1859), p. 162. Google Books.

Henry O'Neal Turner: Thompson Cooper, *Men of Mark: A Gallery of Contemporary Portraits of Men Distinguished in the Senate, the Church, in Science, Literature and Art, the Army, Navy, Law, Medicine Etc.* (Cleveland: 1887), p. 810. Google Books.

"I could do my own writing, unbeknown to the overseer, and carry my own pass": Randolph, *Sketches of Slave Life*, p. 16.

"I wrote passes for the other men on the place": Thompson, *The Life of John Thompson*, p. 108.

"forge passes for herself": William Wells Brown, *Narrative of William W. Brown: An American Slave* (London: 1849), p. 144. Google Books.

"can write a pretty hand": Woodson, *The Education of the Negro*, p. 84.

"forging three passes": Drew, *The Refugee*, p. 185.

"ordinance of 1850": Trexler, *Slavery in Missouri*, p. 182.

VII. The Effects of the Laws

"beat drums or blow horns": O'Neall, *The Negro Law of South Carolina*, p. 26.

"Barbados, as early as 1676": Diana Paton, "Witchcraft, Poison, Law and Atlantic Slavery," *The William and Mary Quarterly*, Vol. 69, No. 2 (April 2012), p. 251.

"as they may judge necessary": Stroud, *A Sketch of the Laws Relating to Slavery*, p. 189.

"Georgia passed the same law in 1770": *Charleston Digest*, Appendix, p. 33; Clark *et al.*, *Interesting Memoirs and Documents*, p. 239.

"not at any particular hour, but at sun-down": Stuart, *Three Years in North America*, p. 493.

"teach such orphan reading, writing or arithmetic": Benjamin Watkins Leigh, William Waller Hening and William Munford, *The Revised Code of the Laws of Virginia: Being a Collection of All Such Acts of the General Assembly, of a Public and Permanent Nature as Are Now in Force; with a General Index.: To Which Are Prefixed, the Constitution of the United States; the Declaration of Rights; and the Constitution of Virginia* (Richmond: 1819), p. 269. Google Books.

"by 1850, perhaps one-half of free blacks in the South were literate": John Cummings and Joseph A. Hill,

Negro Population in the United States, 1790-1915 (New York: 1968), p. 405. Google Books.

"banned dancing": Henry, *The Police Control of the Slave in South Carolina*, p. 48.

"The editorial listed the evils": *Id.*, p. 51.

"the stakes belonged to any white person": *Charleston Digest*, p. 57.

"St. Louis made it unlawful, after 9:00 p.m., for slaves or free blacks to attend 'any ball, dance or religious assemblage'": *The Revised Ordinances of the City of Saint Louis, 1835-1836* (St. Louis: 1836), pp.124-125. Google Books.

"half of the slave states had laws banning the teaching of reading and writing to slaves": Morris, *Southern Slavery and the Law*, p. 347.

"all the letters that passed between us": David W. Blight, *A Slave No More: Two Men Who Escaped to Freedom: Including Their Own Narratives of Emancipation* (Harcourt: 2007) (Narrative of former slave John M. Washington), p. 172. Print.

"areas for Missus to preach or teach": Rohrer, "Slaveholding Women and the Religious Instruction of Slaves in Post-Emancipation Memory."

"a major crime": John Anthony Scott, *Hard Trials On My Way* (New American Library: 1974), p. 68. Print.

"all Negro schools were clandestine": Richard Robert Wright, *A Brief Historical Sketch of Negro Education in Georgia* (Savannah: 1894), p. 28. Google Books, and available at the Library of Congress: http://tinyurl.com/sketch989

"I never saw but one that could write": Clark *et al.*, *Interesting Memoirs and Documents*, p. 80.

"greatest number of readers": Jones, *The Religious Instruction of the Negroes in the United States*, p. 115.

"not one in fifty": *Collection of Writings on the Slavery Question* (New York: 1838), p. 28. Google Books.

"5,000 of 400,000": Parsons, *Inside View of Slavery*, pp. 248-249.

"more scared of newspapers than they is of snakes now": Georgia Baker. Georgia Slave Narratives.

"white men's book": Abigail Mott, *Narratives of Colored Americans* (New York: 1875), p. 78. University of North Carolina - "Documenting The American South", 1999. <http://docsouth.unc.edu/neh/mott/mott.html>.

"the mental capacity": Henry Bibb and Lucius C. Matlack, *Narrative of the Life and Adventures of Henry Bibb, an American Slave* (New York: 1850) ("Henry Bibb"), p. 102. Google Books.

"the price of a slave in New Orleans, hired out as a waiter to a hotel, was higher for slaves who could read and write": Stuart, *Three Years in North America*, p. 229.

"slaves reading newspapers": Wade, *Slavery in the Cities*, p. 174.

"education became a police matter": Woodson, *The Education of the Negro*, pp. 80-86.

"buy a spelling-book": Benjamin Griffith Brawley, *A Social History of the American Negro; Being a History of the Negro Problem in the United States, including a History and Study of the Republic of Liberia* (New York: 1921), p. 134. Google Books. .

"Attitudes favored illiteracy": Jones, *The Religious Instruction of the Negroes in the United States*, p. 115.

"not one of them had the mere rudiments of education": *Id.*, p. 171.

"not a dozen colored people able to read and write": Wright, *A Brief Historical Sketch of Negro Education in Georgia*, p. 21.

"North Carolina's experience": Bassett, *Slavery in the State of North Carolina*, pp. 98-101; Caldwell, *Slavery and Southern Methodism*, p. 32; p. 37.

"inquisitorial visits": William Drayton, *The South Vindicated from the Treason and Fanaticism of the Northern Abolitionists* (Philadelphia: 1836), p. 203. Google Books.

"religion without letters": Woodson, *The Education of the Negro*, p. 179.

"The goal of Christianity was to make slaveholders more godly": David Brion Davis, *Slavery and Human Progress* (Oxford Univ. Press: 1984), p. 166. Print.

"dancing, fiddling, flirting, smoking cigars, and abusing Abolitionists": James Stirling, *Letters from the Slave States* (London: 1857), p. 150. Google Books.

"only one married couple could read": Parsons, *Inside View of Slavery*, p. 236.

"a quarter of whites could not write their name on marriage certificates": Special Report of the Commissioner of Education on the Condition and Improvement of Public Schools in the District of Columbia (U.S. GPO: 1871), p. 803. Google Books.

"Two or three ladies": Moncure Daniel Conway, *Testimonies Concerning Slavery* (London: 1865), p. 5. Google Books.

"after whipping us we would be sent back": William Ferguson Goldie and Isaac D. Williams, *Sunshine and Shadow of Slave Life Reminiscences as Told by Isaac D. Williams to "Tege"* (East Saginaw, MI: 1885) ("Sunshine and Shadow"), p. 66. Google Books. .

"patrols and mobs": Woodson, *The Education of the Negro*, p. 197, footnote 2.

"We used to slip off in the woods in the old slave days on Sunday evening way down in the swamps to sing and pray to our own liking": Alice Sewell. Missouri Slave Narratives.

"469 free blacks and slaves were arrested at one church meeting in 1817, followed by an arrest of 144": Henry, *The Police Control of the Slave in South Carolina*, p. 141.

"Two slaves were convicted": Trexler, *Slavery in Missouri*, p. 180.

"Sometimes the paddyrollers catch us and beat us good but that didn't keep us from tryin'": W.L. Bost. North Carolina Slave Narratives.

"there is preaching only once a fortnight, or once a month, and then perhaps only one sermon": Jones, *The Religious Instruction of the Negroes in the United States*, p. 176.

"considered best to disband schools": Harrison, *The Gospel among the Slaves*, p. 93.

"suspending their schools": Clarke *et al.*, *Interesting Memoirs and Documents*, p. 250.

"the cold shoulder": Harrison, *The Gospel among the Slaves*, p. 370.

"how we served God": Belinda Hurmence, *We Lived in a Little Cabin in the Yard* (J.F. Blair: 1994), p. 4 (narrative of former slave Charles Crawley). Print.

"to prevent slaves from meeting for religious worship": Bibb, *Henry Bibb*, p. 32.

"Bibles and Hymn books were particularly mentioned": Weld, *Testimony of a Thousand Witnesses*, p. 51.

"a mystery to the white brethren": Louis Hughes, *Thirty Years a Slave. From Bondage to Freedom. The Institution of Slavery as Seen on the Plantation and in the Home of the Planter* (Milwaukee: 1897), p. 53. Google Books.

"negro pew": Clarke *et al.*, *Interesting Memoirs and Documents*, p. 280.

"after the whites had partaken": Bassett, *Slavery in the State of North Carolina*, p. 52.

"accompanied by the ridicule of others of the society": Collins, *Practical Rules for the Management and Medical Treatment of Negro Slaves in the Sugar Colonies* (London: 1803), p. 217. Google Books.

"churchgoing by whites": Parsons, *Inside View of Slavery*, p. 259.

"not a settled minister of the gospel": *Id.*, p. 259.

"everyone able to go about, can hear preaching once in two weeks, or once in a month at farthest": Estes, *A Defence of Negro Slavery as It Exists in the United States*, p. 100.

"religion was of great importance in the management of slaves": Andrews, *Slavery and the Domestic Slave-trade*, p. 189.

"a pro-slavery tract": Estes, *A Defence of Negro Slavery as It Exists in the United States*, p. 101.

"The people spend the Sunday more in amusements and in shopping": Stuart, *Three Years in North America*, p. 239.

"Miss Bessie went and all the white folks went to see their negroes go under": Easter Lockhart. South Carolina Slave Narratives.

"the blacks believe the damned among the negroes to become monkeys": Julius Froebel, *Seven Years' Travel in Central America* (London: 1859), p. 220. Google Books.

"saved more rice for massa": Harrison, *The Gospel among the Slaves*, p. 210.

VIII. Searches and Punishments by Patrollers

"free coloured man must not carry a cane": Chambers, *American Slavery and Colour*, p. 123.

"The principal object of such visits is to terrify the slaves": Andrews, *Slavery and the Domestic Slave-trade*, p. 102.

Ida Henry and Sallie Carder: Oklahoma Slave Narratives.

Hattie Sugg: Mississippi Slave Narratives.

"The patrols used the element of surprise when searching a home": Hart, *The American Nation*, p. 102.

"all at once here come them paddyrollers": Henry Green. Arkansas Slave Narratives.

"see that none of the inmates left": Jacobs, *Incidents*, p. 100.

"broken crockery, old shoes": William Howard Russell, *My Diary North and South*, Vol. 1, (Boston, 1863), p. 147. Archive.org.

Huts; "beds were collections of straw and old rags": Henson, *Father Henson's Story of His Own Life*, p. 8.

"this here yellow gal's got letters!": Jacobs, *Incidents*, p. 100.

"whiling away their time with the help of a fiddle and a bottle of whiskey": Richard Hildreth,. *The Slave: Or Memoirs of Archy Moore* (Boston: 1840), p. 71. Google Books.

"chiefly from their drinking too much liquor": Henry, *The Police Control of the Slave in South Carolina*, p. 34.

"Georgia's law against drunkenness on patrol": William A. Hotchkiss, *A Codification of the Statute Law of Georgia, including the English Statutes of Force: In Four Parts. To Which Is Prefixed, a Collection of State Papers, of English, American, and State Origin; Together with an Appendix, and Index* (Savannah: 1845), p. 818. Google Books.

"a company of licentious and inebriated young men": Andrews, *Slavery and the Domestic Slave-trade*, p. 102.

"the patrollers were not all that reliable": Aptheker, *American Negro Slave Revolts*, p. 304.

"left ear cut-off": George Washington Williams, *History of the Negro Race in America from 1619 to 1880* (New York: 1883), p. 295. Archive.org.

"removal of one or two front teeth": Weld, *Testimony of a Thousand Witnesses*, p. 83.

"a strong and sound tooth was extracted": Clarke, *et al., Interesting Memoirs and Documents,* p. 134.

"held up by the patrol as a terror to the slave": Henry, *The Police Control of the Slave in South Carolina*, p. 121.

"This is not by any means an uncommon punishment": Brown, *Slave Life in Georgia*, pp. 88-89.

"as a northerner recounted": Parsons, *Inside View of Slavery*, p. 158.

"with bells on": Charles Ball, *The Life of a Negro Slave* (Norwich: 1846), pp. 133-136. Google Books.

IX. Forms of Resistance by the Slaves

A. Real-World Punishments for Secretly Learning To Read or Write and Examples of Resistance

"When I can read my title clear": Lowery, *Life on the Old Plantation in Ante-Bellum Days*, p. 85.

"seditious skill": Monaghan, E. Jennifer. "Reading for the Enslaved, Writing for the Free: Reflections on

Liberty and Literacy." *American Antiquarian Society* 108, no. 2 (January 1998): 309.

"they would almost cut your throat": Various Authors. William Still, *The Underground Railroad.*

Carrie Davis, William Henry Towns, Lucindy Lawrence Jurdon and George Young: Alabama Slave Narratives.

James Lucas and Alex McCinney: Mississippi Slave Narratives.

Solomon Northrup: Various Authors. Northrup, *Twelve Years a Slave.*

Susie King Taylor: Susie King Taylor, *Reminiscences of My Life in Camp with the 33d United States Colored Troops, Late 1st S.C. Volunteers* (Boston: 1902), p. 5 and p. 8. Archive.org.

Thomas Jones: Jones, *The Experience of Thomas H. Jones, Who Was a Slave for Forty-three Years* (Boston: 1880), pp. 13-20. Archive.org.

Reverend W.E. Northcross: Alabama Slave Narratives.

Jenny Proctor: Texas Slave Narratives.

"wrote in the sand": Raboteau, *Slave Religion*, p. 241.

Elijah Marrs: Elijah P. Marrs, *Excerpts from Life and History of the Rev. Elijah P. Marrs, First Pastor of* Beargrass Baptist Church, and Author (Louisville: 1885). University of North Carolina at Chapel Hill, "Documenting The American South." http://docsouth.unc.edu/neh/marrs/marrs.html

"most allus called on by de others for preachin'": Elisha Doc Garey. Georgia Slave Narratives.

Sam Johnson: Raboteau, *Slave Religion*, p. 234.

"he used to spell it out": Elizabeth Hyde Batume, *First Days Among the Contrabands* (Boston: 1893), p.7. Archive.org.

Mary Gladdy: Georgia Slave Narratives.

B. The Danger of Prayer and Prayer as Resistance

Anderson Edwards: Texas Slave Narratives.

Ida Henry: Oklahoma Slave Narratives

"slaves always had to carry a li'l piece of paper": Sarah Felder. Mississippi Slave Narratives.

Mingo White: Alabama Slave Narratives.

Sally Carder and James Southall: Oklahoma Slave Narratives.

Richard Caruthers and "hush harbors": Raboteau, *Slave Religion*, p. 218.

"'Lord, deliver us from under bondage.'": Raboteau, *Slave Religion*, pp. 216-217.

C. Physical Resistance To The Patrols

Resistance to slave patrols, in general: Genovese, *Roll, Jordan, Roll: The World the Slaves Made*, pp. 637-648.

"Easter night": Steward, *Twenty-two Years a Slave, And Forty Years a Freeman*, pp. 28-29.

"some of them got burnt in the face and neck badly": Henry Clay Bruce, *The New Man - Twenty-nine Years a Slave, Twenty-nine Years a Free Man* (York: 1895), p. 98. Google Books.

"ashes could be tossed": Willie Williams. Texas Slave Narratives.

"Sometimes a stout man will fight his way through": Drew, *A North Side View of Slavery*, p. 249 (narrative of Philip Younger).

"fodder stack burned" and Princess Anne County: Aptheker, *American Negro Slave Revolts*, p. 148.

"the colored people cut off their horses tails": Smith, *Fifty Years*, p. 17.

"Uncle Peter Clay": Trexler, *Slavery in Missouri*, p. 183, fn. 41.

"Grapevines": Louise Pettis. Arkansas Slave Narratives.

"commence to sing comic songs": Smith, *Fifty Years*, p. 19.

"patrol members could be killed": Mandy Cooper. Kentucky Slave Narratives.

"stretch clothes lines": Drew, *North Side View of Slavery*, pp. 156-157 (narrative of former slave Francis Henderson).

"Patter-rollers carried a crooked handle-stick": Henson, *Father Henson's Story of His Own Life* (narrative of Benjamin Henderson), p. 175.

"big iron pot at the door": Minnie Fulkes. Virginia Slave Narratives.

"pray around a tub of water": Fannie Moore. North Carolina Slave Narratives.

"turn a pot down so as not to let the sound go far": Berlin, *et al.*, *Remembering Slavery*, p. 65 (narrative of former slave Levi Pollard).

"put their faces down in a dinner pot": Eliza Evans. Oklahoma Slave Narratives.

"slaves were forbidden to own their own dogs": Brown, *Narrative of William W. Brown, An American Slave*, p. 153 (citing Mississippi statute).

"name of some creditable white person": *Charleston Digest*, p. 75.

"Mississippi, in 1822, authorized patrols to kill all dogs kept by a slave": T. J. Fox Alden and J. A. Van Hoesen, *A Digest of the Laws of Mississippi: Comprising All the Laws of a General Nature, Including the Acts of the Session of 1839* (New York: 1839), p. 675. Google Books.

"Old Bill Rolling Pin": Linda Goss and Marian E. Barnes, *Talk That Talk: An Anthology of African-American Storytelling* (Simon & Schuster: 1989), p. 488. Print.

"This is often done by the first one arriving breaking boughs from the trees, and bending them in the direction of the selected spot": Randolph, *Sketches of Slave Life*, p. 68.

"palm it off" as a pass: Bruce, *The New Man - Twenty-nine Years a Slave, Twenty-nine Years a Free Man*, p. 96.

"towards midnight theses gentlemen grow cold": Ball, *The Life of a Negro Slave*, p. 188.

"the most usual and accustomed road": Randolph, *Sketches of Slave Life*, p. 164.

"the conjure": Henry Green. Arkansas Slave Narratives.

"greased his feet with rabbit-grease": Albert, *The House of Bondage*, p. 22.

"red pepper": Drew, *North Side View of Slavery*, p. 186 (narrative of former slave John Warren).

"plenty pepper with them to rub on the bottom of their feet at nights": Narrative of L.B. Barnes, *quoted in* Fox-Genovese, *Within the Plantation Household: Black and White Women of the Old South*, p. 321.

"red onions and spruce pine": Williams, *Sunshine and Shadow*, p.10.

"bed of jameson weeds": Lewis W. Paine, *Six Years in a Georgia Prison: Narrative of Lewis W. Paine, Who Suffered Imprisonment Six Years in Georgia, for the Crime of Aiding the Escape of a Fellow-man from that State, After He Had Fled from Slavery* (Boston: 1852), pp. 22-23. Google Books.

www.ingramcontent.com/pod-product-compliance
Lightning Source LLC
Chambersburg PA
CBHW070528220526
45467CB00003B/902